I Will Be Found

I Will Be Found

"...COME NEAR TO ME, AND I WILL COME NEAR TO YOU."

A Daily Prayer Journal and Spiritual Guide

Marcie Julian Temple

I dedicate this prayer journal to
Emily Drew, William Allen
and Grace Anne,
without whom I would not have continued
searching and seeking.
Thank you for
opening my eyes, my heart, and my soul,
for the longing to understand
Perfect Love.

Introduction

✳ ✳ ✳

"I WILL BE FOUND" EXPRESSES my walk, my journey, from relying on self-will to relinquishing control and surrendering, in exchange for God's good and perfect will for my life.

This is my journal full of prayers, seeking and study. It's my road map to a more fulfilling and intimate relationship with God. It was begun when I was in the dark, wanting and needing help. Knowing deep, deep down inside that there was something I was missing, something that could free me from myself.

I visualize myself climbing out of a deep dark tunnel and when I began writing this journal I had begun to climb, I had begun seeking light, seeking God like never before because I was alone. I had no one to turn to for help, I was trapped with myself and the only way out was death or God.

This journal became the catalyst for my freedom and I can't help but share it with others. I realized at times that God was talking to me; His Holy Spirit was giving me direction, and hope, encouragement and grace. His words have been highlighted throughout this book, the words of God that I was blessed to receive and to hold on to, words that got me from one day to the next.

I began sensing God's light through spending time with him, in a quiet space, praying and meditating, then writing and seeking. I was climbing out of this deep dark tunnel, one that I dug for myself because I wasn't nurtured as a baby, I was emotionally abused by my mother and believed a lot of what she said to me was truth. I was told that I was no good, that I wasn't worth a penny, that she would give me away but nobody would want me, that I should be ashamed of myself. I grew up feeling less than and believed that all I had to offer the world was "pretty." I was caught up in dysfunction and had learned unhealthy ways to view the world and lived each day by following what the world said would make me happy and successful and fulfilled.

I was lost.

But slowly and very surely, I was brought to my knees again and again, beginning with the birth of my first daughter, Emily. Holding her in my arms my first thought was "how could a mother not love her daughter?" I felt a love for this baby that I had never felt before, a love that helped me begin to understand the love that God has for me. To believe that God loves me more than I could love my own baby was unimaginable to me. And so I vowed that I would be different, that I would be a good mother for my daughter and provide her with what I didn't receive as a child from mine, and so began my story of healing of replacing the untruths and ugliness, with God's truths and God's light and most of all His LOVE.

This journal begins with me, ragged and threadbare, weak and haggard, looking up to see a light beckoning me to hang on, to dig in! I kept hearing, **"I love you with an un-imaginable love Marcie, I AM your Father, I love you and you WILL be found by ME!"**

I am trapped inside this bleak, cold, abyss, I'm tired and hungry, lonely and afraid, but I somehow have the will to look up, to begin.

I envision my daughters saying "love us, mommy, love us the way you wanted to be loved." So I dig my fingernails in, take a step, then another, and as I climb, I surrender my self-will with each step to something bigger, to God Almighty, who is far more capable of pulling me out of this hole, this hole that He had no part in digging.

He reaches out His hand and I take hold of His, and my steps become easier and the light becomes brighter, and suddenly, I'm standing outside and the world is changed. I lift my hands to the heavens, and I surrender myself, my little bitty self will in exchange for God's WILL and freedom in knowing that He really IS in control and He really WILL take care of me forever and ever and not just in the morning but all day long and into the night!

I WILL be found! And I was!

You can be too! Be willing! Begin seeking something bigger than we, a force that cannot be reckoned with because this force is God, our Creator.

I've always had the sense that something I couldn't see or touch was with me. As a child, I spent a lot of time alone, but I don't ever remember feeling alone. There was always something there that would talk to me and with whom I would speak, who would care for me and keep me safe. I remember knowing that it was God at the time, but as time went by, this "knowing" was overshadowed by hurt, pain, loss, abuse and ugliness.

I was "saved" when I was 22. I went home with a couple from my church, sat at their kitchen table and said the Prayer of Salvation. I remember being both overwhelmed and overcome with hope, and realized that I had once again tapped into this presence that I had known so well as a child. I sensed it then and know now this is the Holy Spirit. I was overwhelmed with joy because my sin had been weighing so heavy on me and I knew I could start over, that I had been washed clean, completely forgiven by this deity.

I felt relieved and loved and glad to be back in touch. I stayed connected with God by going to church, checking in on occasion, especially when times seemed tough, and proclaimed myself to be a Christian. That's about as deep as it went. At the time, I didn't really understand what it meant to be in relationship with God, and I was too busy to figure it out.

When I turned thirty, I began seeking God like never before. My friends would ask, "What do you mean by seeking?" and this is what I came up with, I began seeking something bigger than myself, something better. I just knew there had to be more to my life than this struggle, this keep up with the Joneses mentality that I had been held captive by all of my life.

My daughter, Emily, was now 3, and I was pregnant with my second child who we learned was going to be a boy. My water broke when I was at 36 weeks when I was trying on shoes at a shoe store. I went to the hospital, and within hours, I lost my baby, Will, because of a placental abruption. It was horrifying and traumatizing and I was told that I was lucky to be alive, and so I piled this on top of everything else and kept going.

I became pregnant again the following year, and on the very day I lost Will, I began to bleed and I knew in my heart that this baby was gone too. I was in the hospital having a D&C on the very day we had buried Will the year before. I was so angry with God, and cried and pleaded and begged to know "why?"

The following year, I miscarried another baby, and then I gave up. I gave away anything in my home that reminded me of a baby and decided to begin to pick up the pieces of my family and my marriage and ultimately of myself. The depression I felt was palpable, the insides of my arms, where a baby rests when they are held close, would throb and ache and I would massage them with my fingers to ease the pain.

One day, I wanted to die, the hurt was too much and I screamed and cried and begged God to show up and ease my pain. If He were really with me, I needed to FEEL Him, or I couldn't live another day.

I can't tell you how I knew that He was there, but just like when I was younger, I knew He was. He calmed my soul and re-assured me, just as He had told me since I was a little girl that everything was going to be okay. And I heard Him and I believed Him and I received His blessing of hope. **"You're going to be ok."**

We all know what happened next, we were given grace in more ways than one. I don't know when or how Grace was con-ceived because intimacy was not high on our list at the time, but God's grace was given to me again in the form of a beauti-ful baby girl, and of course her name had to be the same.

I continued seeking God after Grace was born. My mar-riage was in the ditch, I was still struggling with the death of Will and I needed to understand the dysfunction I had en-dured from my family of origin. I was essentially a single mom, my husband was rarely home and when he was, there was no interaction. I was numbed out and needing help. I've realized since becoming a therapist that I was deeply depressed during this time. I was having regular thoughts of suicide and continuous thoughts that were self-degrading. I had developed enough understanding to realize that praying and studying relieved my pain for a while. My eyes had been opened just enough that I kept going, kept seeking His light. I wasn't doing it for myself at this point, I was doing it for my babies, my girls because I knew that they needed me, because I was going to be the mother to them that I never had. I was going to fight with every thing I had to provide them with the love and nurturing that I never received.

Oh my GOD was it a fight! But thanks to my GOD I WON! My girls are incredible and I know that the only reason this is true is because God in ME saved me from myself! He freed me and allowed me to be a GOOD momma! He brought me into His light and when you know what it feels like to be in His light, there's no turning back!

Through my searching, I kept journals. I didn't write in them every day, nor was I careful to keep them nice and pretty or straight. I wrote in some of them only a few times, and in others, every page is covered. The point is, I wrote what I was feeling and what I was experiencing, and the common thread that I see in all of them is God and a belief in a higher power, something bigger, what I didn't understand is just how HUGE the power of God really IS!

Throughout this seeking, I grew to understand the grieving process and accepted the death of my son. I was able to forgive my mother and father for their shortcomings as parents. I went through a divorce and came out the other side with no hatred or bitterness. I developed an understanding of the importance of giving up control over my children to a God who is far more capable than me. I began to look at myself in the mirror and stop blaming others for my issues, and began taking responsibility for the part I played in the failure of my relationships. I quit my job and went back to school full time and became a therapist, and the seeking just grew and flourished, and saved me again and again and again, until ultimately, I was able to forgive myself.

I am forgiven and so are you. Until we understand what this means, we will forever be a prisoner of our own making, in our own minds, allowing others to keep us behind the bars with no key to unlock the door.

I can give you the key, God gave it to me, and I want to share it with you, but you are the one who will need the courage to first take the key from me, put it in the lock, unlock the door, and then step outside. Freedom is beckoning and it's up to us to answer the call!

It is a choice, one of the most important decisions I've ever made! In order to understand forgiveness, it takes discipline and courage, perseverance and strength, all provided us by Him who is WAY more powerful than we!

This journal is a tool to help you begin seeking the Will of God for your life. It's meant to open your eyes, your heart and your mind to something more powerful than you could ever imagine. God is all-powerful! He wants what's best for me and for you. He loves us because God IS love, and therefore so are we! We are made in His likeness, and we must learn to surrender our will for His if we want to live out our time on earth being who He created us to be! I hope you will awaken to a living God who is with us and wants us not only to live freely but also to thrive!

I hope this journal will be the catalyst for you to write your own story of seeking to know the truth. God really is Good! If you choose to seek Him, He will be found by you, and more importantly, as you read and pray and study and seek, I can promise you this:

YOU WILL BE FOUND!

God with us

✳ ✳ ✳

EVERYWHERE

TAKE SOME TIME TODAY TO sit down and relax. Closing your eyes, count your breaths as you breathe in and then again as you exhale. Begin visualizing a place that brings you peace. I will share one of mine with you:

I am sitting Indian-style on a sandy beach at the ocean's edge, my hands upturned on my lap. I can feel the ocean breeze on my body, tossing my hair, caressing my face. I can feel the warmth of the sun on my skin, its rays on my eyelids, knowing that if I opened my eyes, the light would be so bright I would have to close them again. I smell the ocean breeze, its air infiltrating every pore of my being. I breathe in more deeply as I sense its pureness. I imagine it cleansing my body with each breath, taking out any impurities that might be present. I visualize a rainbow with all its many colors, resting on the fingertips of my left hand going over my head and touching down onto the fingertips of my right hand, and this makes me smile. I sense a connection with the ocean, and just as the waves come in and touch the sand, they are touching my soul and pulling a part of me back with its tide.

I am ONE with it, and it is ONE with me. I have a sense of peace that washes over me that cannot be denied, and I know I am whole, I am fully connected, ONE with the Universe, and ONE with God.

God with us, and I know that God IS.

God IS EVERYWHERE.

This is Goodness and this is Light!

Let's get moving! There really is no time like the present!

This is simple instruction to help you move through this journal and into a deeper more meaningful relationship with God, our Father, the ONE who created the world and ALL that is in it!

Read the journal entry for the day. One day at a time is enough. Dwell on it's meaning throughout the day and begin bringing your mind's focus from self to God. This takes practice but I know that you can do it!

Because this is a journal, there's no rhyme or reason given to format. Some days include scripture; some days don't, but open your Bible in honour of God anyway! Read a few scriptures and dwell on them throughout the day. This is truth, this is goodness, this is LIGHT!

"Finally, brothers and sisters, whatever is true, whatever is noble, whatever is right, whatever is pure, whatever is lovely, whatever is admirable--if anything is excellent or praiseworthy--think about such things."

Philippians 4; 8

What are you thankful for today? Take the time to write about it! Thankfulness will change your life!

"Give thanks in all circumstances; for this is God's will for you in Christ Jesus." I Thessalonians 5; 18

Look for goodness, look for light; it's always here, even in the darkest of circumstances.

"You will seek me and find me when you seek me with all your heart. I will be found by you," declares the Lord, "and will bring you back from captivity."

Jeremiah 29; 13-14

(Pray) "O Lord, not my will but THINE be done."

"Father, if you are willing, take this cup from me; yet not my will, but yours be done."

Luke 22; 42

January 1st

* * *

I AM THANKFUL FOR YOU, that you are reading this, and that you are seeking God. He is here with us, right now. This IS truth, our soul and God's Holy Spirit longs for us to know this.

Thank You, God that you are here, that you are ready to direct our steps beginning with today, the first day of the New Year!

We praise you and thank you for LIFE, for your truths and for your son, Jesus, who came to earth and set the example for us to live by.

Help us, O Lord, to remember these two truths as we begin the New Year. First, help us to treat others as we ourselves wish to be treated and second, may we continually ask ourselves, "What would Jesus do?"

Not my will, but Thine be done.

Matthew 7:12
John 13:34-35

January 2nd

*   *   *

THANK YOU LORD, THAT YOU are right here, right now! Thank you for today and for the gift of LIFE! This year is yours, and I commit myself fully to your will for my life. Therefore, I surrender self, I lift my hands to the skies and pray to You, O Lord, "Not my will, but Thine be done."

Things are looking UP! I challenge you where you are sitting, or even better, step outside into the miraculous world that God created for us to live. Close your eyes, lift your hands to the sky and thank Him!

Luke 22:42

Goodness and Light:

To surrender in spirituality and religion means that a believer completely gives up his own will, and subjects his thoughts, ideas and deeds to the will and teachings of a higher power.

January 3rd

✳ ✳ ✳

THANK YOU, O LORD, FOR you are our source of strength and our Father who will not disappoint, who will not waver. We pray together, "Thy will be done," help us to be pleasing to you.

Walk outdoors and lift your hands to the heavens and pray, "Thy will be done" and mean it with every fibre of your being. KNOW that God sees you and hears you, and reaches out to touch your fingertips. Feel His presence.

God with us.

Matthew 6:10
Romans 5:5

January 4th

✳ ✳ ✳

Dear Lord,

I'M RELEASING ALL MY HURT, I'm giving it to you because I know that you are far more capable than me in dealing with it! We thank Thee for Thy divine presence, for Thy infinite wisdom, for loving us despite our weaknesses, for forgiving us because of our humanness. We thank Thee, O Lord.

Give God your struggles and hand over your pain. He will take it from you and strengthen you.

Colossians 3:13
Psalm 118:1

Goodness and Light:

To live in LOVE is to forgive and be forgiven (forgive ourselves). To open our souls and surrender it all to Him with open arms. "O to Thee, my precious Saviour, I surrender All".

Hear our prayers, O Lord.

January 5th

* * *

THANK YOU, O LORD, FOR instruction, for rest. Thank you for discipline, for you are "the Way, the Truth and the Life." We are your children, and we remain thankful. Continue to lift us up and energize us, O Lord.

Praise Thee, Father. Praise Thee, Lord.

Praise Thee and thank Thee, for our hope is in you.

Psalm 86:12
Psalm 25:4-5

January 6th

∗ ∗ ∗

I AM SO THANKFUL FOR you today, that you are continuing to search out and seek a more meaningful relationship with God. He is with us always! He is everywhere! God IS spirit, God IS love, "we cannot escape the LOVE of God."

"We are not human beings having a spiritual experience. We are spiritual beings having a human experience." – Teilhard De Chardin

Psalm 139:7-12
1 John 3:24

Goodness and Light:

Our souls are where the Holy Spirit resides, and if you've ever felt the Holy Spirit, you may have an idea of what I'm talking about. It's when you know that you're pleasing God. You are doing exactly what He wants you to do, and He's letting you know it. It's such a feeling of sheer ecstasy, and there's nothing else like it. Being in touch with the Holy Spirit (connection between us and God) has to be what can only be described in human terms as pure bliss, contentment in the NOW, being fully present, inexplicable happiness, being in the perfect WILL of God the Father.

Eckhart Tolle says, "there are no words in our present day vocabulary to describe this state of being."

It is perfectly INDESCRIBABLE.

January 7th

* * *

*WE ARE IN NEED OF **nothing but the TRUTH.***

Dear Lord,

We cannot perceive our own best interests. We are tired of try-ing to make our lives work, struggling and striving to meet our own needs. Our way is simply not working and it's far too ex-hausting to continue in the same direction, not experiencing the life you promise. We are willing to LET GO of our way. We are finally ready to surrender and "LET GO AND LET GOD."

We pray, "Thy Will be done," knowing that you want us to live in your perfect peace your perfect LOVE. We want to hear You, O Lord. We want to be closer with you, in relationship with you, "on earth as it is in heaven." Open our minds Lord, guide us to your light. Thank you for Your Grace and the understanding that it is completely undeserved. "For Thine is the Kingdom, and the Power, and the Glory, Forever and Ever.

Matthew 6:9-13

Goodness and Light:

To surrender means to yield power; to give up completely or agree to forgo especially in favor of another; to give (oneself) over to something (as an influence.) To surrender is willful acceptance and yielding to a dominating force and their will.

January 8th

* * *

Dear Lord,

We pray for wisdom and your perfect Will be done.
Where would you have us go?
What would you have us do?
What would you have us say? And to whom?

We are thankful that God loves us.
We are thankful that we love God.
We are thankful that this is ENOUGH.

God IS.

Romans 5:8
James 1:5

January 9th

WE ARE THANKFUL THAT WE can be thankful.

We are connected to the greatest Source of light in the universe, the Creator of the universe! How overwhelming is this: To KNOW that we have the awesome opportunity to continue moving toward His light, towards His love.

Ephesians 5:20
James 1:17

January 10th

* * *

WE ARE THANKFUL THAT WE are forgiven. Lord help us to forgive, to fully understand that "as long as I am having any thoughts of unforgiveness towards anyone (judgment, criticism, or condemnation) I am hindering progress in myself."

Colossians 3:13
Ephesians 4:32

Goodness and Light:

Here's the thing: When we move towards God, He moves toward us, and if we pay attention, He gives us exactly what is needed at the time to keep going. Believe and receive this truth.

January 11th

* * *

THANK YOU; LORD, FOR PRAYER, one way in which to honour you, to speak to you, to hear you. God loves me. God loves you. This IS enough.

Philippians 4:6-7
1 Thessalonians 5:16-18

Goodness and Light:

Prayer is communicating with God. I don't feel the need to be in a quiet place, or have a certain routine such as bowing my head and closing my eyes, holding hands or following a script. I just talk to God like I'm talking to a best friend. I have since I was little. I know that He hears me and this is all that matters. Sometimes I'm sure I look as though I'm talking to myself, and for years, I thought I was. I would say, "you're gonna be okay," all day long some days, because it comforted me.

I recognize now that this was God in me, comforting me, loving me through. We can talk to God anytime, all day every day if we want; this is what "pray without ceasing" means to me.

January 12th

* * *

THANK YOU, O LORD, FOR opening our eyes. Let's Wake UP! Today is the day to choose to receive His blessings, gifts wrapped up in wisdom and LOVE. God, you are the Way, the Truth and the LIFE! What more is there? We seek your Will for our lives, the only WAY. I choose LOVE. I am compassionate, creative and loving. You are all-powerful and my Source of strength.

Thank You for this day, Lord. Help us to hear you and to follow your Light, your Love. Help us to free ourselves-, from ourselves, knowing that your love is the answer and we are all connected, equal in your eyes.

John 14:6
Matthew 21:22

Goodness and Light:

Equality is an understanding that there's nothing, or no one in the Universe more or less important than you. If you don't feel equal: Inferiority/Superiority=FEAR.

January 13th

* * *

THANK YOU, LORD, THAT WE have nothing to fear with you at the helm of our ship, our Captain. You promise to never "leave us nor forsake us" and your Word is Truth.

Hebrews 13:5
Isaiah 41:10

Goodness and Light:

Fear or oblivion is a scary word and one I don't like to say or even write or think about. Oblivion, is the scariest most torturous place one could ever be, a living hell, a no-man's land, it's an illusion created by us in our minds. It's giving power to darkness and ignoring the light.

We must open our eyes and understand the POWER our minds have. FEAR is the reason why it is of the utmost importance that we learn to discipline our minds.

One definition of fear is the acronym: "false evidence appearing real". It's an illusion, one with which we could torture ourselves on a daily basis with excessive worry and anxious thoughts. If we aren't careful, our entire lives can be based on fear, on the "idea" that something negative may or may not occur.

The bigger picture here is that FEAR is NOT OF GOD, and so therefore, it has no business occupying our minds or even one second of our time. If we are overcome by fear, then we are living closed-minded, having little or no faith in the truth that our God has overcome fear and darkness for us.

We have been set free from fear. The chains have been loosed, through the LOVE of God. If we can't believe this truth, then we must work on our faith and decide if we want to live a life of fear or a life of love. It's a choice. Believing and receiving God's LOVE and releasing fear is like a groom lifting the veil of his bride and finding his beloved; or when a plane takes off on a cloudy day, ascends into the heavens and all of a sudden reaches the light of the sun, the vast blueness above the shroud of gray clouds.

God's love is a gift, ready to be opened, and from this amazing gift comes another gift, and another, and another.

January 14th

* * *

THANK YOU GOD, THAT YOU are here, the living God who will never leave us or forsake us! You are Goodness, You are Light; there is NO darkness in you. This is how I see, this is how I know. Our prayers connect us; our meditation brings us closer so that we can hear your voice. This is our way to receive your guidance and instruction. Your Word says "you will know them by their fruit." I will walk in love, joy, peace, patience, kindness, goodness, faithfulness, gentleness and self-control. You love us more than we can imagine, and this is ALL we need to know. Help us to love others, help us to be powerful, creative and compassionate. All of these things, we can be, through trusting in you, our Rock, our Redeemer, our Atonement, our Saviour.

God IS and WAS and FOREVER WILL BE!

Galatians 5:22-23
Deuteronomy 31:6

January 15th

WE THANK THEE, O LORD.
God is with us.

I AM here with you right now!
I AM present, NOW, TODAY!
Fight the good fight of FAITH!
"Take courage. It is I, do not be afraid…"
God with us. God with you!

Matthew 14:27
Matthew 1:23

Goodness and Light:

What if all that we had left in this world when we woke up to-morrow morning, were the people and things that we thanked God for throughout our day today?

January 16th

* * *

THANK THEE, O LORD, FOR opening my eyes.

Spend time with me in stillness and silence, seek my will for your life and fill your mind with my promises. Dwell on My goodness and relax in my arms knowing that you can trust Me. Have faith dear children I AM the GREAT I AM!

Believe and receive this truth!

Exodus 3:14
Matthew 17:20

Goodness and Light:

"I am as close to God as I want to be." Joyce Meyer

January 17th

* * *

THANK YOU, LORD, THAT I am yours and yours alone.

Speak through me; allow me to be your vessel. You are my Rock and my Salvation. I am connected to you. I "live and move and have my being" because of you. I pray, "Your Will be done" this is why I AM, and this is what You Will.

Peace be with you.

Acts 17:28
Psalm 62:6

January 18th

* * *

ALL IS WELL; THANK YOU, O Lord, that you are my constant companion.

Believe and receive my message, this promise.

Psalm 46:10
Matthew 28:20

January 19th

* * *

I AM THANKFUL FOR FAITH, the sunrise this morning and for freedom that comes from Your Word, your Promises. I visualize your unending abundance, far above what's beyond my imagination. There is no end to Your Spirit, which encompasses ALL.

You, O Lord, are Mighty to save!

2 Corinthians 5:7
Romans 10:17

"Expect GREAT things. Expect GREAT things!"

Hebrews 11:1 reads: "Faith is the assurance of things hoped for; perceiving as real fact what is not revealed to the senses." (sight, taste, sound, touch and smell)

Goodness and Light:

We must understand that in order to grow our faith, we must believe in and hope for, that which is invisible or unseen.

January 20th

***

I AM THANKFUL TO BE awake! To KNOW that God is with me, and that I am pleasing Him! This is all that matters! What a relief knowing this IS! Freedom through Christ!

Praise God, Hallelujah!

Galatians 5:1
Romans 8:28
Jeremiah 29:11-14

Goodness and Light:

God IS and this is all that matters.

This is the day when I opened my devotionals and my bible and the words came alive. This is the day that I knew without a shadow of a doubt that I was a child of the Most High God, the Light of the World, the Ruler of the Universe. The words rang clearer than a bell, and it was like the curtain was lifted and revealed the Wizard of Oz--but yet I knew that there wasn't a wizard, I didn't need one anymore.

I had received God's Word, and all that I had to do was seek His face, and He did exactly what He said He would do. "Seek Me and you will find me when you seek me with all your heart, and I will bring you back from captivity." and that is exactly what God did, and I recognized that I was captive to myself, and the beliefs of others that I had been inundated with since I was a child. FREEDOM RINGS! And on this day, it rang ever so LOUDLY. I was AWAKE, and my life would never be the same!

A personal note:

If you've ever had the pleasure of experiencing being near the ocean, you can't help but sense its massiveness and enormous power. Seeing the majestic mountains with all of their vastness and strength, the painted sky with no end in sight, looking down at the pieces of a puzzle with its parts so delicate and fragile; these marvelous wonders of the world help me to KNOW without a doubt in my mind that I am only a speck of dust on the horizon, one that will be here and gone in an instant!

January 21

* * *

THANK YOU, O LORD, FOR "It is well with my soul." I praise Thee all day long. Use me, O Lord, not my will, but Thine be done.

Luke 22:42
Psalm 35:28

Goodness and Light:

Soul in my own words: The definition in and of itself cannot be contained; the soul cannot be reined in. "My soul is the truth of who I am in God's eyes, my spirit, unending and infinite, the essence of who I am. The soul is I, in spirit form; it is purity, simple and sweet, and holds all of the spiritual fruits: love, joy, peace, kindness, goodness, faithfulness and self-control.

January 22

* * *

THANK YOU FOR THE DISCIPLINE to seek your face and for your strength to guide me through, keeping me awake and aware, un-distracted. "You will uphold me with your righteous right hand."

Seeking to know you more.

Mark 4:13-18
Isaiah 41:10
Matthew 6:33

January 23

* * *

THANKFULNESS IS A DISCIPLINE THAT leads to a life of excellence, the life that God willed for you and me, a life serving Him. To be in relationship with God, in a close, personal relationship, it is PARAMOUNT that we spend time with Him, disciplining our minds, meditating on and studying His word, His promises.

Be still and pray.

Psalm 92:1-5

Goodness and Light:

If we don't learn to discipline ourselves, we won't have a close relationship with God. One of the keys to His wonderful Kingdom is discipline. Disciplining ourselves yields much fruit and freedom for our lives, and the rewards far exceed the time and effort. Take my word for it and keep the faith. It's truth and nothing but the truth.

Let's practice a visualization exercise: Close your eyes and imagine the biggest, most beautifully wrapped box you can think of. Mine is 5 ft. tall by 4 ft. wide and is a beautiful shade of blue with a satin white ribbon. Now, walk over and untie the ribbon and lift the top of the box off. Immediately, pretty gifts in boxes of all sizes and colors begin to rise, floating out of the box, each one more beautiful then the next, and you know that you get to open each and every one of them, for they are ALL just for you.

This is what God's love does: It's the gift that keeps on giving gifts, unending gifts, forever and ever. Just a few of the gifts you will receive are clarity of mind and peace of mind. As if this weren't enough, as we continue seeking Him, he continues filling us up to overflowing with gifts, ones that won't wear out, be forgotten or trashed, lost or re-gifted.

January 24th

* * *

I AM THANKFUL THAT I know that fear does not come from God. "For God hath not given us a spirit of fear…" We must resist fear. Fight fear by replacing fearful thoughts with God's promises and love. Fight! In Jesus name! Anger is an expression of fear; ask yourself, "what am I afraid of?" All fear is selfishness and unbelief that God will take care of you. God is my refuge and fortress! I have nothing to FEAR!

2 Timothy 1:7
Psalm 46:1-3

January 25th

* * *

THANK YOU, O LORD, THAT you have given me all that is needed to strive for excellence in my life, a life spent serving You, a life spent seeking Your Will, the only life that can satisfy.

1 Peter 4:11
James 3:18

Goodness and Light:

Sew excellent seeds and you will reap an excellent harvest.

January 26th

* * *

I AM THANKFUL, O LORD, for you and Your Son, Jesus, and the Holy Spirit. For without Your Holy Trinity, I couldn't live in peace and know to receive them, and rest in knowing that I have nothing to fear, and nothing to prove.

I am thankful that your love covers ALL. I cannot remove myself from your love. It is all encompassing, every breath that I breathe, I breathe it in, your love, covers me. Thank You Lord, that you are everywhere and everything. God IS, and for this I am thankful.

God IS.

Habakkuk 3:17-18

*Believed to be the strongest affirmation of faith in all scripture

January 27th

* * *

O LORD, THOU ART HERE. Let us feel Thy nearness.

Psalm 118:1
Psalm 89:15

Goodness and Light:

I am thankful and filled with joy when I say that the "realness" of how fragile life on earth is, and how quickly the years go by have become very real for me. This realization has been beckoning for a while now, and I am forever grateful that my eyes have been opened. My priorities have changed completely, and I am free to enjoy my days, one at a time, knowing full well that I'm not promised a tomorrow. I wake up feeling thankful, and go to bed feeling the same way. I am in love with God, with my family and my friends. I know that forgiveness is necessary and is the "golden key" we must use to unlock living a fuller existence. I also know that the God of the Universe is everywhere, and in everything, and that He loves us more than we will ever be able to understand.

I am so thankful that I see the fragile-ness and love in every-one, and that I can sit with no judgment, realizing that I am neither beneath nor above anyone. We are all on the same plane; all connected and beautifully and wonderfully made for God's Glory!

Believe and receive this truth!

January 28th

* * *

I SEE YOUR LIGHT SHINING more brightly everyday! Draw me in; keep me moving toward your love, toward your light.

Goodness and Light:

If we are growing closer to God, spending time acknowledging Him, honouring Him with our time and our prayers and our minds, we will begin looking forward to connecting with Him as often as possible. This time will become the most important part of our day, our quiet time as many call it. We will see that to begin our day this way, sets our mind on our Creator, and goodness and love, despite how we may be feeling when we awaken in the morning.

There've been many mornings when I've awakened and felt physically bad or just had negative thoughts in my mind. Immediately, as I've grown and studied, I've learned to "go to" thankfulness and just begin thanking God that I'm awake, for one more day of LIFE, for a job to wake up to and a family to reach out to and love.

Instantly, my mind is transformed to a better place, refreshed and renewed, ready to begin my day with my God. If we are growing in relationship with God, these things WILL take place. God promises, "Come near to me, and I WILL come near to you." And He WILL!

January 29th

* * *

THANK YOU, O LORD, FOR your Holy Spirit which is called by many names: the Counselor, the Spirit of Truth, the Spirit of Life, the Spirit of Wisdom, our Comforter.

The Bible reads in John 14:26, "But the Counselor, the Holy Spirit whom the Father will send in my name, will teach you ALL things and will remind you of everything that I have said to you. Peace I leave you, my peace I give to you. I do not give as the world gives. Do not let your hearts be troubled and do not be afraid."

God IS LOVE IS God.

Isaiah 9:6-8

January 30th

* * *

THANK YOU, O LORD THAT I can fully trust in you. You will never disappoint me; you will never leave me nor forsake me. You are the reason that I am, for it is through you "we live and move and have our being."

God IS.

Acts 17:28
John 16:33

January 31ˢᵗ

* * *

THANK YOU LORD, FOR YOUR promise that if we continue to seek You, You will be found by us. I find comfort in your word. I believe completely in your promises. I pray "Your will be done." I pray for my complete obedience. I know that I am yours and this is enough.

God IS love IS God!

Amen

Goodness and Light:

I am thankful for you, the reader, that you are continuing to seek God, I can assure you, you will be astonished and amazed at what you will find along the way.

Always remember this truth:

"You will seek me and find me when you seek me with all your heart." Jeremiah 29:13

Write about it

Write about it

February 1

* * *

GOD IS OUR "EVER PRESENT help" *ever-present means ALWAYS present. It is us that walk away from God; he remains constant beckoning our return.*

Hope in ME and you will be protected from depression and self-pity. These behaviors are not of God these behaviors are not light. You must avoid them at all costs and I will show you how. "Remain in me" "seek me with all of your heart, with all of your strength with ALL of your soul and you will find me."

Remain in me.

Psalm 46; 1
John 15; 4
Jeremiah 29; 12-14

February 2

* * *

IMAGINE THAT HOPE IS A beanstalk (*Jack and the Beanstalk; one of my beloved fairytales that my grandmother would read or recite to me at bedtime*) made of gold that reaches as far as the eye can see into the skies, the heavens. We are drawn to it because of its beauty and our wonder of what lies at its end. We begin climbing and notice that the higher we go the more at peace we feel, our burdens lightened, heaviness made up of guilt and self-degradation that used to penetrate us is being replaced with goodness, joy and peace. Our faith is strengthened with each step we take climbing higher and higher and higher.

1 John 1; 5
Galatians 5; 22-23

Goodness and Light:

Now listen to this and I mean believe it with every fiber of your existence. Heaviness is not of God. Cling to HOPE and God's light will reach you through the darkness. "for in Him there is NO darkness."

Come on get higher, keep climbing!

February 3

* * *

THIS IS FOR YOU A gift from God, if you're feeling guilt it is of your own doing. You are forgiven, believe in and receive my forgiveness.

Mathew 21; 22
Psalms 103; 12

Goodness and Light:

Dwell on God's promises and he will get you through it, not only will He get you through it, He will make you better. He will color your world.

February 4

✳ ✳ ✳

THANK YOU JESUS, OUR EVER-PRESENT, all knowing all encompassing help and savior. Thank you for pulling me to you, for magnetizing my spirit, for holding me near. Thank you for helping me to see that your promises are true, that they define truth. You are truth.

I pray that each second, I will surrender and that I won't have to be so thoughtful about it, that it will become like breathing.

Become my breath O Lord, become my everything. I am so thankful that my eyes are opening to the magnitude of your majesty and your infinitum. What can be keeping us from wanting to know you more? This is a question worth pondering and answering swiftly so as not to miss out any longer.

Job 32; 8
Zephaniah 3; 17

February 5

* * *

THANK YOU O LORD THAT your promises are ringing loudly and truth is what I see. **"I am with you."** You really will NEVER leave us nor forsake us, how many times do we need to read this to believe it?

Goodness and Light:

How did Jesus stay nourished? He spent time with his father in prayer and meditation, he went away to a solitary place with no distractions, no people pulling him away, begging, grasping for anything and everything he had to give. How he must have been tired at the end of the day. Can we imagine a day in the life of Jesus? The patience and just utter ignorance and pomposity he had to overlook or just disregard. It's because he knew, this wasn't for him to judge. He could only set the example and teach. This is the reason he came to walk among us.

He stayed focused on his job, his purpose, his passion, his goal. He was here to save, here to teach, here to set an example for His Father. The time spent with God, the Father kept him filled up, motivated, intact, loved. He knew that he was here in body to take care of business and then he knew he would be returning from whence He came. This is what our mission statement should be; this is the truth of our existence on earth. To follow the example of Jesus, to stay in tune with God and His Will for us while on earth.

What keeps us from keeping our focus on the DIVINE?

Distractions keep us from it; feelings keep us from it, not living in the present, not living in the HERE and NOW keep us from it.

How do I control this from happening? I ask god to help me, to take over, to protect me.

Protect me from myself O Lord, Heed my cry and save me; lift me up and out of this place and set me free upon a rock. I want to see you more clearly. Save me O Lord.

"You will seek me and find me when you seek me with all your heart I will be found by you declares the Lord and will bring your back from captivity."

Jeremiah 29; 13

And He WILL! Believe and receive this truth!

February 6

∗ ∗ ∗

THANK YOU LORD FOR LIFE and today, for right now! Continue to open our eyes, so that we may live the rest of our days knowing that you are in control of our seconds and this knowing is the golden key to our peace of mind our letting go our complete surrendering to you.

Goodness and Light:

Our eyes truly are windows to the soul. There's nothing sadder than to see blankness, indifference, anger, ego, struggling, sadness or hurt, through one's eyes. But to see enlightenment, hope, love, caring, and happiness, there's nothing like seeing darkness turn to light in the eyes of a fellow human being. It's one of the loveliest sights I've ever seen, likened to a sunset or sunrise, or a storm rolling in from the ocean. And to see this in a child's eyes is perfectly indescribable, it makes my heart sing!

Thank you Lord for journaling, it's been a mainstay my entire life and a way to free myself from myself. It allows me to see you more clearly. Thank you Lord I pray that nothing will interrupt my time with you, my life is forever changed, I feel as though I've been set free and I'm sure that I have been.

February 7

∗ ∗ ∗

THANK YOU LORD THAT WE are all here for a reason, to do your Will, to serve a purpose. Thank you for allowing me to let go to recognize, to SEE that letting go of my will is necessary in order for yours to be done. This "letting go" is not possible without seeking understanding and being in relationship with you. It takes time, patience, perseverance and discipline but the rewards far outweigh the effort. Thank you for walking with us Lord even when we stray to the right or the left, you never do, you wait for us to come back every time.

Goodness and Light:

My life has taken on a new meaning, my eyes have been opened and I have been given a gift. This gift is what I believe to be God's Will for my life at this moment. I want to give to others what I wished to receive when I was at my lowest. I have a knowing like never before that this is God's Will for my life, my purpose, my passion. I am thankful and humbled.

February 8

* * *

Awakening

THE WORLD HAS BECOME A canvas, a beautiful painting in motion with the most vibrant and sparkling colors imaginable, like entering the Land of Oz or the chalk art that Mary Poppins and Bert jump into for a Holiday with the penguins. I ALWAYS wanted to jump into those pictures and it's as though I have!

An artist can never capture the radiance of the sky on a perfect day, all of the shades of blue and gray, the light just right, peeping in and out of the magnificent, blustery clouds. I saw a sky today that I don't remember seeing before, and if I had I'd forgotten. I wondered if today was my day to leave this earth if affected me so. I feel like I am feeling the rhythm of the earth, and I am one with it. I sense my connection like at no other time and it's mesmerizing. It's dream-like to the point of driving me to tears more than once.

I wonder, can this really be happening to me? I have this tiny whisper of a thought "don't let me mess this up..." but it's too grand and too powerful and it's not of me and this is the perfection of this happening because it's not me and I KNOW it! It's the divine in me, the perfect the peaceful, the silkiest, softest part of me. One that I can rest in, that I can trust, that I can believe in with everything that I AM. I've been searching for this my entire life, since I was a little girl. I've always known it was there. It always held me close; I could feel it in my deepest, darkest moments. It would talk to me in a whisper and tell me I would be ok, to hold on, that I had a reason to hold on to life. Oh! To be there for others who are in this place! But I know that I can't, they too will have to know that it's not just their souls that inhabit themselves, it's another, greater than them.

February 9

* * *

I LOVE MY TIME WITH my God in the morning, my favorite time of day. This is truly the best time to spend with God, after a good night's rest or a restless night. I look forward each morning to what will emerge from my soul and what I might see and learn.

Spend quality time with me. I will equip you for your day's journey. My being, my Presence is your companion for each step that you take today. Stay in continual communication with me, whispering my name whenever you need to re-direct your thoughts. Focus on Me.

February 10

* * *

THANK YOU LORD FOR THE understanding that we must walk through life aware and awake, paying attention; otherwise we miss out on what you have in store for us. To feel your warmth, to feel your joy, this is what I seek, to be more like you Lord, our infinite King, our Savior.

Goodness and Light:

When I was walking today in the park, a huge crane startled me and took off within 5 ft. of me. Coincidence? I think not! Be aware of what's going on in nature when you are outdoors, you will be amazed!

February 11

* * *

LIVING IN LOVE IS TO forgive and be forgiven, to open my soul and surrender it to Him with open arms. Oh to thee my precious Savior I surrender all.

My trust is in you O Lord, all day long. Praise thee, Father; Praise thee O Lord; Praise thee and thank thee for my hope is in you

I Peter 5; 6-7
Proverbs 16; 9
Psalm 37; 5

February 12

* * *

THANK YOU FOR INSTRUCTION, FOR rest. Thank you for discipline, for you are the way the truth and the life. I am your child and I am thankful; lift me up, energize me.

Jeremiah 29; 14

February 13

* * *

YOUR THOUGHTS ARE HIGHER THAN my thoughts. Your ways are higher than my ways.

Grace is the acceptance of the love of God.

God is but love and therefore so am I.

Goodness and Light:

Every decision you make stems from what you think you are and represent the value that you put upon yourself.

A Course in Miracles: Deciding for Peace

Separate my thoughts from who I am.

A Course in Miracles: A New Beginning

February 14

GOD LOVES ME AND THIS is enough.

This IS truth, this IS light!

You are enough!

February 15

* * *

I AM THANKFUL THAT I can be thankful.

My purpose is being revealed.

We are connected to the greatest source of light in the universe. Continue to move toward Him. He will overwhelm us with His AWESOMENESS!

Goodness and Light:

As long as I am having any thoughts of un-forgiveness towards anyone (judgment, criticism, condemnation) I am hindering progress in myself.

I AM discourses

February 16

✳ ✳ ✳

Let's WAKE UP!

Equality is understanding there's nothing or no one in the Universe more or less important than you.

Goodness and Light:

This IS truth, this IS light!

If you don't feel equal: Inferiority/Superiority= FEAR.

"I AM NOT I." *Juan Ramone Jimenez*

February 17

* * *

WALK BESIDE ME O LORD; fill me up with your LOVE; I am
yours and I want your Will for my life. I am yours and this is
ENOUGH.

February 18

* * *

GOD IS WITH ME.

I AM here with you RIGHT NOW!
I AM Present, Now, Today!
Fight the good fight of FAITH!
Take courage it is I, Don't be afraid."

Mathew 14; 27

February 19

* * *

ALL IS WELL

Thank you O Lord that you are here, you are my constant companion.

"Be still and KNOW that I AM GOD." Psalm 46; 10

February 20

* * *

THE WORD ANEW MEANS, FOR an additional time, again, in a new and different form, to begin anew.

"Expect great things. Expect great things!"

Faith is the assurance of things hoped for perceiving as real fact what is not revealed to the senses.

Hebrews 11; 1

Goodness and Light:

I am thankful for Faith, this morning sunrise and for freedom in your word. I visualize your unending abundance beyond infinity. There is no end, the skies, the oceans, the mountains, the plains, unending abundance.

February 21

* * *

HAVE FAITH LIKE A CHILD'S, just follow ME!
Strive for excellence, just follow ME!
Sew excellent seeds and you will reap an excellent harvest,
when you follow ME!
I will give you confident peace. Trust in ME!
Now is what matters. Serve me well. I AM everything. I AM
everywhere!

Psalm 126; 5
John 16; 33
Psalm 63; 2
Psalm 139 7-10

Goodness and Light:

EXCELLENCE is the state or quality of excelling or being exceptionally good; extreme merit; superiority.

February 22

✳ ✳ ✳

THE MOMENTS GOD REVEALS THINGS to us and we are busy and thoughtless are the moments that can change the course of our lives and keep us from going down a treacherous path of our own making. Pay attention!

Philippians 4; 8

February 23

* * *

I HEAR YOUR SPIRIT LORD speaking to me now. You help me to live my life to the full rather than allowing anything and everything else to cloud my vision. I find rest in knowing that you are the same yesterday, today and forever, unchanging, my mountain, unmoving, unshakeable. You give me a peace that transcends understanding.

Fix your eyes on me...focus on me, the ONE who never changes!

Hebrews 13; 8

February 24

∗ ∗ ∗

I AM WITH YOU NOW and always. Come to me, relax in my Peace. Do not fear, only trust.

Ephesians 1; 17-19

Goodness and Light:

At times I want to know the dictionary's definition of words. When I'm studying in the mornings, reading my devotionals and my bible, I pick out words that stand out to me and look into them further. I look up their meanings and will follow them through the bible. It's just something I do and it's been extremely enlightening at times. I learn a lot by doing this, sometimes right away and sometimes days later.

On this day I read Proverbs 16 and these are the verses that stood out to me.

"How much better to get wisdom than gold to choose understanding rather than silver. " "Pleasant words are a honeycomb, sweet to the soul and healing to the bones."

I hope everyone is able to experience hearing pleasant words today but even better, I hope that everyone is able to experience the gift of speaking pleasantness to someone today.

Another word that caught my attention this week is "Mosaic." The word means that even the littlest stones play a big part. A mosaic is made up of thousands of colorful stones, big and small that make up a beautiful work of art. What color stone are you? And what part do you play in the completed masterpiece, where has the artist, our creator, placed you?

I am a stone that's a pretty turquoise blue, one that you can see through when held up to the light.

February 25

* * *

PLANTING A SEED

I CUT UP COLORFUL PIECES of poster board and wrote, "God is in this place." I planned to drop several of them at all of the schools I visited that day. I frequented schools during this time because I was satisfying my internship requirements to be a counselor. I put a few in my coat pocket and went to the High School to see a client. I was nervous because this was taking me out of my comfort zone and I was afraid someone might see me drop them.

I was told to go to the Library to wait for my client. Upon entering, I realized I was alone. It was filled with a peaceful silence like no other, surreal really. I walked along the rows of books and dropped one of my little treasures. I pictured someone picking it up and using it for a bookmark or showing it to someone else so the thought might enter their being too. "God IS in this place." The simplicity of the task and the magnitude of the words on the cards gave me an adrenaline rush! I'm hoping it brings someone comfort in the very least and as I write this I realize that it already has.

February 26

* * *

FOLLOW ME; TAKE THE HIGH road and follow me, stay close to me, hold tightly to my hand.

Habakkuk 3; 19 The Sovereign Lord is my strength He makes my feet like the feet of a deer he enables me to go on the heights."

When I went to this scripture, first of all I don't think I've ever been to this chapter and second of all I thought it was beautiful. Beautiful enough that I wanted to further understand it's meaning. I read the meaning my bible gives the verse: "gives me sure footed confidence (probably the conductor of the temple musicians; chanted with the accompaniment of instruments; stringed instruments including the harp and the lyre.)

Come what may; pray daily for my gift of faith. Follow me, no matter what; stay close to me and hold tightly to my hand. I will enable you to take the high road to the heights by the renewing of your mind!

Goodness and Light:

I've always admired orchestra conductors and fantasized and pretended to be one. I took ballet for many years growing up and obtained an appreciation for classical music. This music calms me and makes me happy. I close my eyes and use my imagination and see myself as a conductor making all of these talented musicians play together in harmony to the gentle waving of my hands.

February 27

✳ ✳ ✳

Pay attention!

This IS Truth and this IS Light!

Steps that will bring you closer to God and His will for your life:

1) Spend time with God in prayer and meditation, reading, studying and praying. This is what I call seeking.
2) Spend the day focusing on all that is good and worthy, the beauty in the world. It's a choice; don't watch or listen to anything that could pollute the mind, keep it pure and lovely and tender, like a child's.
3) Bring my conscience mind to this day, to right NOW, our senses help with this. This is where God IS, in the present and we must be paying attention to see it. If we aren't living in the present and our focus is on the past or tomorrow, we are missing out on the life God has planned for us. The past is just that, it's passed! All we can do about the past is learn from it! The future is not promised, we never know if tomorrow will

come! "Today is the day that the Lord has made! Let us REJOICE and be glad in it!"

4) Dwell in thankfulness for NOW, today, this moment! Focus on being thankful for what you have not what you hope for!

5) Forgive quickly and constantly so as not to hinder or stain the clear connection to God.

6) Speak God's word to vanish negative/dark thoughts, speak out loud if needed and then believe that God has taken it away. (practice faith)

7) Relinquish control; relax and follow God's lead, He shows us everything, each second of the day! He will give us exactly what we need every single time!

8) Pray: "Use me O Lord I am yours. Your Will not mine be done. I am yours O Lord and this is ALL that matters. I know that you are with me and that you will never leave me nor forsake me!

February 28

* * *

IF WE AREN'T WILLING TO start our days with God, if we can't give Him our time, then we won't come to know him. Let's look at it this way, in simple terms. If you want to get to know someone, you really want to be friends with them; won't we do all that we can to foster this relationship? We call and text them, we go to lunch, we spend time with their families, we recognize their birthdays and anniversary's, we are there for them when times are hard, we talk to them and listen to them and seek to know them better!

Goodness and Light:

"We are as close to God as we want to be." Joyce Meyer

February 29

∗ ∗ ∗

Goodness and Light:

GET A PICTURE OF YOURSELF as a child. I have photograph of my-self at the age of 1. It's black and white and it reflects purity and tenderness. This was me before anyone started telling me what to believe in, before I was told to eat this and not that, before I was told that this family member was good but this one was bad, before I was told that this religion was wrong but mine was right, that I couldn't take communion in this church but I could in that one, that I was middle class and better than some but not as good as others, that I should hang out with this person but not that one. That I had to perform and stand out in order to be loved, that my looks were the only thing that I could depend on, that I wasn't worth a penny, that if I could be taken back from where I came from I would be, but that no one would want me back, that I think I'm so great but I'm not so great. Before all of that, ME, God's child, pure and lovely and unblemished and tender and sweet and smiling, just want-ing to love and be loved.

This is how God wants us, so that He can renew our minds with HIS love and HIS words and HIS promises.

Forget anything anyone has ever told you and know that I love you and will care for you and love you from the ground up. I AM TRUTH and LIGHT and LOVE, follow ME NOW and I will SAVE YOU FROM YOURSELF.

Write about it

Write about it

March 1

✳ ✳ ✳

I HAD TO FIND MYSELF, I had lost my voice, had crumbled inside, I had become emotionally stunted and bruised from being verbally abused because I believed what I had been told. I had to find the hurt little girl who was buried deep inside under all of the sludge and muck and mire and re-connect with her. Once re-connected, I had to lose her again, die to her, and replace her hurt with a foundation of goodness, I had to re-connect to my spirit as a child and re-build with a sure and firm foundation, the LOVE of GOD.

But freedom has found me the chains have been loosed! He did as he promised and brought me back from captivity and set me high upon a rock and I can feel HIM and I can see HIM and I can love HIM and I can rest in HIM. He brings me to tears with His tenderness and grace and hope. My faith cannot waiver now; I am completely covered by an unfathomable love, the love of God.

March 2

* * *

THERE'S NOTHING QUITE LIKE WATCHING someone living their passion. It just feels good, when this is happening, a connection of our souls. That deep, shuttering, longing in our core that we don't feel that often anymore unless we are at a movie that touches us, or at church, or struggling with loss of a loved one or pet or listening to music that touches us deeply. Recall when you got your first kiss? When you fell in love or got some unexpected good news? When you held your first child? These are the times we feel our genuineness, the truth of humanness, and our connection to the universe and to all things, even each other.

This is what we can have everyday if we pay attention to our God and our universe and our passions and our today's instead of our yesterdays or tomorrow's. Today is what really matters. Pay attention! This moment has already passed....

Come on Get HIGHER!

March 3

✳ ✳ ✳

DEAR LORD, I WANT TO go where you want me to BE. I trust you with my day. Help me to listen and to follow. Thank you Father, my rock, my fortress, my HOPE and my PEACE. You are ALL and complete and fill me to overflowing. Make me and mold me in your likeness, transform me and renew my mind. I am yours and this is enough.

Thy will be done.

Where would you have me go?

What would you have me do?

What would you have me say? And to whom?

March 4

* * *

GOD KNOWS US BETTER THAN we know ourselves. He understands us completely and loves us perfectly. His light, his cleansing, his healing, his refreshing, his renewing, his forgiveness, ALL gifts ready to be opened and received by us.

What are you waiting for?

March 5

* * *

IF WE KNOW HIM, WE can't help but exhibit His light, His love.

I am His and this is ALL that matters.

Thank you, Thank you, Thank you!

March 6

* * *

ONE DAY AT A TIME, **TRUST. Be sensitive to the Holy Spirit, responding to its promptings. Trust in me with ALL things deeply depending on my teaching, my promises.**

Listen, trust, obey and claim abundant blessings of Joy, Peace, Patience, Assurance, Security and Health!

March 7

∗ ∗ ∗

Feel me UP, O Lord with your gifts, with your abundance in ALL things. I am open and ready to receive! I will be exalted and I will persevere in knowing you to the utmost while here on this earth.

"Our Father, who art in heaven, hallowed be thy name, they kingdom come, thy will be done on earth as it is in heaven. Give us this day our daily bread and forgive us our trespasses as we forgive those who trespass against us. And lead us not into temptation but deliver us from evil. For thine is the Kingdom and the power and the glory forever and EVER."

Goodness and Light:

I sat with my 98-year-old grandmother, who's been struggling with her health for a couple of years now. It's tough because she can't do the things she used to love. It's tough seeing her sick and weak. I have a sense of unrest as I sit with her. I watched and listened as she sang along with her church service on the radio, "Praise God from whom all blessings flow" and "Glory be to the Father and to the son," her lips barely mouthing the words, her voice inaudible. Then she said the Lord's Prayer along with the radio and in that moment I recognized that she is the reason why I know these songs and the Lord's Prayer.

I sat beside her and read her devotionals to her, something she has done since I can remember, and I felt a sense of distance instead of closeness. I don't understand why unless I was guarding myself from feeling the brevity of the moment. I recognize today what I have wondered for a while now...I have an emotional wall up that is hard to penetrate and I know it will take some work and time before it is shattered.

God sees through it though, I show myself to Him; there are not many others who will see me. I pray my daughters can see through this glass. I think they do, I think they know me and the realness and authentic self, the tender genuine me that lives beneath the strength and hardness of this glass wall that I sit inside for protection.

March 8

* * *

YOU O LORD ARE WITH me. **Never fear or doubt my love, my power. Persistence and patience brings success as defined by me not as defined by the world, success beyond your hopes and dreams. All is well!**

March 9

* * *

I AM OVERWHELMED WITH THANKFULNESS and God's love. I feel as though I'm being cuddled in His arms, one with Him. Despite my circumstances He loves me and wants nothing but the best for me. He is the same "yesterday, today and forever. " Keeping my eyes on Him and moving with the flow of his perfect timing.

In order for it to grow and bloom and reach it's highest potential, the plant must be cared for by the watchful eye of it's gardener.

March 10

* * *

PRAY TO EXPERIENCE THE LOVE of God. Learn to love discipline to know that you are being asked to reach higher. Open arms, open hands, open heart, ready to receive. Be thankful, freedom is ours. Do not be concerned with tomorrow or get stuck in yesterday. Wake up! Abundant life is here today, right now in His presence. Seek Him today and He will be found by you!

March 11

* * *

BE WHAT GOD WANTS ME to BE! Nothing can separate us from your love O God!

Bloom in His presence, Blossom in His LOVE, emerge from the soil and feel His warmth beckoning us to reach our peak through complete reliance on Him. Surrender and know that God will bring you through better than ever! He wants you to shine like the stars! Be brilliant! Fill up with His goodness and light. Let go surrender your life to Him! Fill up with thankfulness. For it is through Him "I live and move and have my being!"

March 12

* * *

I AM THANKFUL FOR TODAY for the here and now for presence. Keep me awake and aware of what is going on around me. This is where God IS. It's very important that I understand present mindedness. It takes practice and perseverance to not be constantly distracted. BE aware, BE awake and BE watchful. God IS truth and can be trusted to meet all of my needs. He will walk me along a path of peace full of light and LOVE. I must pay attention and not be distracted.

March 13

* * *

HOW CAN I WISH TO receive from the world that which I'm not willing to give?

Give unto others what it is you wish to receive from them. Treat others the way you wish for them to treat you. Give what it is you wish to be given.

March 14

* * *

THE DEEPER YOU'RE WILLING TO go in and explore, the more beautiful it becomes, courage and boldness is necessary when seeking the Will of God.

March 15

∗ ∗ ∗

I SIT HERE WONDERING, YOU know my thoughts Lord, how will I make it financially, pay my rent and bills and provide for my daughters? I lay my life at your feet, I have complete faith that you will cover me, that you want what's best for me, that my answer is right around the corner. Help me O Lord to rely on your word and your promises. Forgive me because I am scared and having thoughts that I'm not good enough, that I'm not doing the right things, that I'm not following your Will, that I'm not pleasing you. Help me O Lord, to be completely dependent on you, to trust and do my best with today. Grow my faith O Lord in things that are unseen believing that they will come to me. You have taught me to remain in thankfulness despite my circumstances. I am thankful Lord for all of my blessings of which I know I have plenty, my cup overflows and I know my mind is being refreshed and renewed day-by-day, second by second. I love you Lord, my Father, my rock, my redeemer.

"My thoughts are not your thoughts my ways are not your ways."

March 16

* * *

THANK YOU LORD FOR MOLDING me and making me and refreshing and renewing my mind. I trust completely in you and your majesty, your holiness. I am yours and I will follow you because I want what you want for my life, your perfect Will. In the stillness I will find you through love, faith and perseverance I will become more like you. Thank you, thank you, and thank you for filling me to overflowing despite my circumstances. You are the great I AM and I am your child! Use me O Lord, help me to be sensitive to your spirit and your direction. Thank you for forgiveness, given me daily for doubting for feeling afraid for being human. Thank you for loving me despite my weaknesses. Thank you for opening my heart and soul to receive your LOVE.

March 17

* * *

I STAND IN AWE OF your goodness this morning. My mind is at peace, my soul is at rest, and my body is recovered. I am in awe of you O Lord. Thank you for your discipline, for your constant help, thank you for making me and molding me to be nothing less than excellent!

March 18

✳ ✳ ✳

OPEN MY MIND O LORD to continue to see the unfathomable miracles that you bestow. Thank you for a sensitive spirit, thank you for growing me up, forgive me for resisting and thank you that you will never give up on me. You will never leave me nor forsake me; you are the same "yesterday, today and forever.

March 19

* * *

BEING IN THE PRESENT MOMENT is freedom. Be watchful, He will prepare the way. *This moment, be present. Lift your eyes to the light, feel my presence warm your face. Allow my peace to flow through you, my love to overtake you. Be still, be watchful and the path will be made clear. Thankfulness abounds in a heart remaining aware and watchful.*

March 20

* * *

KINDNESS IS BEAUTIFUL. I MUST make this a daily goal, for we will never know the lives we are touching, God is watching and hoping for us to stand up and be outstanding! He has equipped us with ALL that we need to be loving, caring people!

March 21

∗ ∗ ∗

I READ THAT GOD IS LOVE, the author and perfector of our faith. He never changes he remains the same forevermore. I believe this and I know that I want to be like Him my father, the keeper of my soul.

March 22

* * *

I FEEL YOUR PEACE AND your LOVE. I'm calm, the questions coming to my mind meaning to sway my faith but you won't allow it. You see the BIG picture, scenes I cannot know. I will continue to follow you, holding your right hand, trusting, hoping, and being sure that you have my best interests at heart. I love you Lord, my trust is in you all day long.

March 23

* * *

TRUST HIM. FEAR IS NOT of God.

To love and be loved, to know peace, to experience life to the full, to enjoy and receive the fruits of the spirit, to recognize spirit connection one to the other, this is just part of God's perfect plan for us.

Continue seeking to know the ultimate source of ALL, God ALLmighty! Filling up with goodness and light, letting go, surrendering. To know without a doubt that we are not in control and this is GOOD. Being fully awake and aware.

March 24

✳ ✳ ✳

To SPEND TIME WITH THE God of the Universe, enjoying His presence, honoring him through prayer and meditation, early in the morning, to understand that this is a privilege and necessary to remain in relationship with him and to be in tune with the beat of the Universe! Keep your instrument, your body, your soul in tune by honoring God first thing in the morning and lastly as you fall asleep. Keep him close, He will draw you in!

March 25

✳ ✳ ✳

I AM ENOUGH. I AM God's child. I am free. I am whole. I am spirit. Focus on Him, keep Him close. Be still and quiet and present with Him. He will keep us headed in the right direction, on a straight path to forevermore. **"Be still and know that I am God."** Thank you O Lord, your goodness overwhelms me!

March 26

* * *

LOVE! GOD IS LOVE! GOD remains the same, never changing, forevermore! *"Fix your eyes on me the author and perfector of our faith!" LIVE in my love my truth.*

The birds song stands out in the morning, I have to focus to breathe in the fresh air, out of my nose and mouth, breathing in deeply and feel the air entering and then leaving my body. I see pretty birds without a care in the world or so it seems, happy just to be. The beauty of the full moon, the promise of a warm spring day all of my senses intact and ready to take it all in, how blessed am I? Can I be more thankful? I'm sure that I could be, I will do my best and it has to be good enough. It is good enough.

March 27

✳ ✳ ✳

"Love covers ALL."

To DWELL IN HIM TO seek His face, to live in peace knowing that He is in control. Be thankful for this moment because it already passed, right now is the most important part of the day. Take it in, experience it, and see the world and its wonders unfolding right now. Remain content today, open our eyes to blessings and beauty, love and hope. His grace, God's grace, God IS and we will be continually blessed as we wake up and sense His light, His presence, it's all around us, it's everywhere.

LOVE covers ALL.

Psalm 29; 15

March 28

∗ ∗ ∗

FOCUS, SEEKING HIS LOVING PRESENCE, quietly whispering His name. Trust Him. To know you more, to rest in your holy presence, I see myself amidst the beauty of the world you have created and I am at peace. You are so much bigger than we allow you to be. Open our eyes O Lord!

Lamentations 3 22-26

March 29

* * *

GOD IS PERFECTION. BLESSED ASSURANCE as this is made clearer as we seek to know Him more and more. We belong to him. He created us. Slow down, become one with nature, see him in the stillness. God is everywhere. GOD IS.

March 30

ALL THAT I AM AND all that I will be is because of you O Lord. This day is a gift; each moment that passes is a chance to see you in ALL things. You are everywhere.

God IS.

To wake up, to be thankful, to experience life through the eyes of God, this is my prayer.

March 31

* * *

I AM THANKFUL TO WAKE up and be blessed with today, to experience life, to know that I belong to God and His will is what I seek, His good and perfect will.

" But seek ye first his kingdom and his righteousness and all these things shall be given to you as well."

Mathew 6; 33

Write about it

Write about it

April 1

* * *

LIGHT AND LIFE, OUR GOD encompasses both. God is Life and has given us life as a gift. He is light and illuminates us spiritually as we seek Him and get to know him. He teaches us to listen and to watch, he enlightens us as we follow Him. Thank you God that you are light and in you there is no darkness at all.

John 1; 4
Psalm 36; 9

April 2

✳ ✳ ✳

CLAIM GOD'S POWER OVER DARKNESS; I am worthy of everything, of God's best because I am His child! The belief that I am not good enough is FALSE and darkness. I claim God's power and promise "I am worthy because of Him who created me in his likeness!" God! Who is the same, yesterday, today and Forevermore!

April 3

***

GOD'S POWER IS LIMITLESS; GOD'S love is limitless. *I am goodness, I AM light*. I find security in knowing that in Him "there is no darkness at all!"

April 4

* * *

RELEASING, RELINQUISHING, RELAXING, WRAPPED, SWADDLED, cuddled in the warmth of your arms O Lord. Sensing His presence, the warmth of the sun on my face and body, the light in my eyes. The sounds of spring, the wind, the bird's singing joyfully caring less who hears. The grand finale a cardinal coming so close I could look in its eyes and see its coat of many different shades of red, it's markings so poignant, so symbolic.

Tears warm my face as I am deeply experiencing the security and love from my maker. Serenity is mine because He loves me and I am thankful.

April 5

* * *

I ONCE WAS LOST BUT now am found, was blind but now I see. God IS in this place. I am loved. I am worthy. God believes in me and I am His. I am special and unique, one of a kind! I have a purpose. I am a piece of God's puzzle, a part of the mosaic of LIFE! I belong.

April 6

* * *

REST IN MY PRESENCE. I will direct your path. The space between the past and the future this is where I am.

Goodness and Light:

I'm recognizing and realizing that we are so small in relation to the size of our universe, and then to think of the immenseness of our God in comparison although in actuality the two cannot be compared. God is everything, the minuteness of the human mind can't conceive of His power. And we think we are in control? I want to surrender my smallness and depend on the Creator to captain my ship. He is far more capable then me and I KNOW it. I'm thankful for this understanding, this gift.

April 7

I WATCH IN HOPE FOR the Lord. I wait for God my Savior. My God hears me and knows what is best for me.

Micah 7; 7
Micah 6; 8
April 6

Goodness and Light:

I had a dream last night and I was told I had one wish for anything my heart desires. Without hesitation, my wish was to know you (God) better, and it's true, if I could have anything in the world today, right now, it would be to know my God.

April 8

✳ ✳ ✳

Our weaknesses reveal His strengths. To come to a place where we only have God is the most powerful place of all. We can't see this until we are there, the loneliest, hardest; weakest moment in our lives is our chance to see Him more clearly.

When we are weak, He is strong.

Cling to truth, cling to God.

April 9

* * *

SEEKING TO KNOW YOU MORE, to reflect you. I am weak but you O Lord are my strength. You have built me up from a seed to a sapling, nourishing me, watering me with your word and your promises. Grow me up O Lord; teach me to bloom in the light of your love.

April 10

∗ ∗ ∗

I'M ALL IN. MY DARKNESS turns to light. You're showing me that "I can do ALL things through Christ who strengthens me." I am weak in my humanness but I am strong with you. Reliance on God is what He wants and then our potential is unlimited because we are connected to the source of everything. To rely solely on God, to know that this is the goal, the ultimate prize, the pinnacle of success, to KNOW this is where complete freedom lies. Seek to know with all of your heart with all of your strength and with all of your soul. Give it your all, everything that you can muster.

I'm all in.

Isaiah 20; 15
Isaiah 26; 3

April 11

* * *

OPEN THE DOOR OF YOUR cages and feel the softness of the wind on your face, the tickle of your tears. Warm, slowly moving down from lashes to cheek to lips and tasting their salty goodness, body relaxing, letting go, surrendering to the freedom that we are divinely loved.

We are His beloveds.

April 12

✳ ✳ ✳

GOD'S PRESENCE BRINGS PEACE. My love is limited. God's love is limitless. Joy, Peace, love, gifts given for seeking, for following, for understanding. Life ANEW, basking in God's promises. All is well.

Thank you Lord for everything, for peace, for love, for hope. Watching the birds this spring, their song so lovely, their flight so effortless, can they know joy? They appear joyful and care-free, but they have a schedule to maintain so they trust, they know to respond to your promptings.

Nature in all of its glory responding to the rhythm of the earth, waiting for us to play our part in it's score, written and conducted by the master conductor, Creator of ALL that was and IS and IS to come!

April 13

$*\ *\ *$

I DID MY BEST AND this is enough. Thank you that now I know. Thank you for opening my heart, my soul, and my eyes to see you, to know you more.

"Give thanks in all circumstances for this is God's will for you in Christ Jesus."

Thank you for making me a mom. Thank you for Emily and Will and Grace and the other baby's I lost and will see again when I see you. Thank you for the love of a child to its mother, thank you for the love of a mother to her child. This love, to me, must resemble your love to us yet I know that your love far surpasses what my mind can conceive. This realization that you love us more than we even love our children is BIG. I know that it takes time to understand and to receive this love, to know that we are your children first, we are your beloveds. The love of God cannot be reigned in.

I Thessalonians 5; 18

April 14

* * *

CONNECT TO GOD, THE SOURCE of all that is good. *"I am with you to the ends of the earth."* God with us. Seeking takes effort and discipline and action. It's making time for stillness and quietness, which enables us to hear spirit. I awaken and thank Him for today and then allow thankfulness to overflow my mind, my being. I try hard not to allow distractions; television, music or social media to interrupt or take the place of my morning ritual of spending time with God. I know that the clearer my mind is the more I will be open and ready to receive and learn.

April 15

* * *

EXPAND OUR VISION O LORD; I continue to hear "limitless." He IS
therefore I AM. My needs are met; I just must believe and receive His blessings. Thank you Lord. I'm willing to follow, lead
me O Lord in your strength.

April 16

*** ✳ ✳ ✳

TWO CARDINALS FLEW RIGHT IN front of me and I knew it was you, reminding me to stay present, watchful, and peaceful. The rain beginning to fall giving the earth it's daily bread, it's sustenance, allowing me to be a part of it, briefly, instead of feeling like I was getting wet, I was thankful for the moment. I wanted to see the birds again but the rain came harder and so I recognized I had seen what I should. I am thankful for an open mind and an open heart.

April 17

∗ ∗ ∗

To know you more, this is my prayer.

Be watchful and alert, love others and trust. I will guide the seconds of your day.

April 18

* * *

REST AND RENEW YOUR MIND, regain awareness of my continual presence and constant direction. I know no limits, I shower you with supplies, be watchful.

April 19

* * *

FOCUS ON FREEDOM, THE ONLY way to truly live. Freedom of country, freedom of mind, freedom to be who you are meant to be, freedom to live and love, freedom to BE, who I created you to BE through ME.

April 20

* * *

CONSTANTLY CLAIMING PERFECT FREEDOM. "YOU will keep in perfect peace, those whose minds are steadfast on you."

Imagine the ripples of goodness, a kind word spoken can accomplish. One of the greatest things I've learned this year is that giving to others what I most need, fills me up!

Treating others how I wish to be treated. If there's a question of right or wrong, the best way to decide is to ask myself, "would I be ok if another did this to me?" The answer comes quickly, the truth of the matter, there's nothing quite like being honest with ourselves. The truth is if we can't be honest with ourselves, if we can't love ourselves, how can we be truthful and loving towards others?

April 21

Goodness and Light:

TODAY I SAW A CHAINSAW started up and then began whacking away at some beautiful red tip photinia and I was disturbed, it was done only because the bushes had begun covering the walk and had to be swiped out of the way when walking by. I looked at these bushes the next morning, all gapped up and mutilated. Their pruner assured me, "it's ok, they will grow back." These bushes drew me to them and I saw a weed had begun taking them over. I began pulling the weed away from the bushes. I realized that if this "pruning" hadn't taken place I wouldn't have seen the weed that had quietly but most assuredly begun to strangle these beautiful bushes. I pulled and tugged and stretched as high as I could, scratching my face, hands and chest, doing everything that I could to free these bushes from this weed. When I had done all that I could I stepped away, sweaty, my hands blistered and hurting. I realized I would need a tool stronger than my hands to finish the job; the weed had taken root in places and was stronger then what my hands could handle.

The next morning, I walked out and saw a part of this weed peering at me again and I reached to pull it and as I did, I noticed that it was dying and was given peace that I had done what was needed to save these bushes.

Sometimes pruning takes place and the results may not look pretty at first, it may bring to light other issues that the plant is having so that the gardener can come in and see what needs to be done to gently but most assuredly care for and nourish the plant back to it's original beauty. It is likely the plant will even be more beautiful and healthy than ever before. In order for it to grow and bloom and reach it's highest potential, the plant must be cared for by the watchful eye of it's gardener.

April 22

* * *

I FIND YOU NOW EVEN amidst the clamor and hurriedness of the world. Things tempt to distract me and at times silence and stillness evade me but, You are here and so am I and I sense your nearness, the indwelling of your spirit and I know I can rest in a haven of your peace, rooted in love, showered in Grace.

April 23

* * *

TRUST AND BE AWARE, WALK in faith and you will find me.

Proverbs 3; 5

April 24

✳ ✳ ✳

EACH MORNING AND EVENING TOO, I walk out and look over these bushes, the weed is quite evident to me now, it sticks out and I can purposefully grab it and pull it away. I look at the root from whence it came and it is weeping sap and I know that in order to assure it's not returning I will need to dig down and pull it from it's foundation, from the soil, which was only doing, it's job by nourishing it. I feel lighter as I watch the bushes become untangled from this weed. I feel as though I'm freeing them from a certain but slow death. It's almost like they are thanking me and giving me hope that they will show me the fruits of my effort next spring. The mangled mess of weeds lying on the ground, brown and crunchy, getting in my way as I work on the bushes, still. I'm ready to rake them up and throw them away. I'm ready to let them go.

John 15; 2
John 15; 5

April 25

* * *

IF I DON'T TAKE TIME to spend seeking God in quiet stillness; I will not come to know him and experience His gifts; If I'm unable to understand forgiveness, I'm only depleting my own spirit, not the one who I feel has wronged me. When I allow myself to be offended, I am weakening my own spirit not the spirit of the other; I am in fact just like them. The high road becomes easier once taken because my spirit is lifted and filled instead of emptied and needy. Without God, none of this is possible; with God "ALL things are possible."

Mathew 19; 26

April 26

* * *

*Be vigilant in guarding your **thoughts**.* Remain alert to choices, continually aware, remaining in His peace, leaning on Him for strength and being thankful always.

Be joyful always, pray continually, give thanks in all circumstances for this is God's WILL for you in Christ Jesus.

I Thessalonians 5; 16-22

April 27

* * *

Just know that there is a battle of the mind, trust in me and be not afraid, focus on my word, keep it close for I am your peace. Guard your thoughts, ask the Holy Spirit to control your mind and life and peace will follow.

"Guard your hearts and minds in Christ Jesus."

Philippians 4; 7

April 28

* * *

*LOVE AND TRUST. LIVE CLOSE **to me, opened and focused**.*

The Holy Spirit is sovereign and we must learn to listen and discern when God is speaking or when darkness is creeping in...

John 1; 5

April 29

* * *

RELAX IN HIS LOVE AND He will accomplish mighty things through you. I am his beloved child. Stay close to God, he will fulfill your needs, His purposes WILL be accomplished.

Psalm 50; 1

April 30

✳ ✳ ✳

YOUR WILL BE DONE. MY trust is in you all day long. Growing in faith, complete trust, confidence and assurance.

"Love the Lord your God with all your heart, with all your strength and with all your soul."

1 John 1; 5

Goodness and Light:

"Do not fear."
I choose LOVE.
"Love your neighbor as yourself."
I choose LOVE.
"Judge not lest ye be judged"
I choose LOVE.
"Forgive as you have been forgiven."
I choose LOVE.

Write about it

Write about it

May 1

* * *

FOCUS ON THE GOOD IT is all around us. See it, observe it, and embrace it, mind, body and soul. I am thankful and grateful for forgiveness and LOVE. Help me to move forward to grow, to know, your good and perfect WILL.

Romans 12; 2
Colossians 3; 2

May 2

* * *

FEELING LOVED BY MY LORD, strengthened by His word, in awe of His presence, comforted, peaceful. " A peace that surpasses ALL understanding..."

Philippians 4; 7

May 3

* * *

YOUR WILL BE DONE O Lord. I am yours. Through you I "live and move and have my being." I am not I, I am yours. I am thankful, humbled and grateful. Keep me here O Lord. I want to stay here. God, you are here, in this place and you wholly love us. Your light shines in the darkness and gives us a beacon to follow, always. May we follow your light, your love even when the way seems dark, you are here.

Acts 17; 28
1 John 1; 5

Goodness and light:

If we are to reflect the ONE who made us we are to love one another.

May 4

* * *

THE STILL QUIETNESS OF THE morning, refreshed from a good night's rest. Reflecting on the weekend and how thankful and grateful I am that God IS and forever will BE. I am releasing my will for His; Freedom through Christ, true and enduring.

Proverbs 8; 17
Galatians 5; 1

May 5

✳ ✳ ✳

BE PRESENT, THIS IS WHERE God IS. God is truth, God is light. My trust is in Him who will supply all of my needs abundantly, for I am His child, His beloved child.

May 6

* * *

TRUST HIM AND HIS LOVE. Praise Him forever.

God with us.

To grow and develop spiritually, in relationship with God, I must be strenuously involved in the process of seeking and persevering. Not because of doubt or anxiety but because of pure reverence and a singleness of purpose in response to the grace of God.

May 7

* * *

PEACE BE STILL. INCREASE YOUR vision, open your thought processes, have courage and grow. Understand the bigger picture and recognize my truths and believe them. You should know that when you seek me I will be found by you. It's my promise and it IS my WILL.

"Come near to me and I WILL come near to you"

May 8

* * *

I AM ONLY HUMAN BUT my God is not. Slow down, get quiet in His presence, and receive the peace only God can give. It's God's peace, which surpasses all understanding.

Philippians 4; 7

May 9th

* * *

I AM THANKFUL FOR A good night's rest, Lolly Gee our dog, Grace and Emily, for peace, understanding and most of all for LOVE. Praying for a sweet friend who is struggling, sending love and light energy her way, may she be open and receive it. May she wake up and sense goodness that surrounds her, may your spirit O Lord touch her.

Feeling blessed, loved and filled because I am well loved. For it is "through you I live and move and have my being." Your will be done. Thank you Lord. Amen

Acts 17; 28

May 10

* * *

BE STILL BEFORE THE LORD and wait patiently for Him. God with us, always and forever. Amen

May 11

* * *

I AM THE GREAT I AM. I am everything and everywhere. Covering you in LOVE. You will return to me. Seek my presence.

May 12

* * *

DEPEND ON ME. COME NEAR to me.

To get to a place of trust and knowing, when I read the bible, I believe it, it comforts me and gives me hope, it relaxes me and continually reminds me that the God of the Universe is in control, not me, thank goodness! Read and believe, know and trust.

Hope, faith, Love and peace abound in our hearts and minds when we surrender our way for the way, the truth and the LIFE.

May 13

* * *

ALWAYS DO MY BEST TO set a good example for God, always! No matter where I am or what I am doing God is there, there's no hiding away.

We cannot hide from the love of God.

May 14

* * *

LIVING IN THANKFULNESS AND GRATITUDE for LIFE and the ONE who gave it.

May 15

∗ ∗ ∗

TO EXPERIENCE ABUNDANT LIFE FREELY given, isn't this enough? To know that the creator of life is the same yesterday, today and forever, shouldn't this give us peace? We are assured of these things over and over and then He tells us "I am with you forever and throughout eternity." I am the Alpha and the Omega who is and who was and who is to come, the Almighty. My trust, my faith, my hope lies with Him.

May 16

∗ ∗ ∗

THINK, THINK, AND THINK, WE have to discipline our thoughts, as written in this verse.

"Finally, brothers, whatever is true, whatever is noble, whatever is right, whatever is pure, whatever is lovely, whatever is admirable, if anything is excellent or praiseworthy, think about such things. Whatever you have learned or received or heard from me, or seen in me, put it into practice. And the God of peace will be with you."

Philippians 4; 8-9

Goodness and Light:

Our thoughts influence our lives! What a person allows to occupy his mind will sooner or later determine his speech and his action. The combination of these virtues is sure to produce a wholesome thought pattern, which in turn will result in a life of moral and spiritual excellence.

May 17

* * *

NATURE IS GOD'S NURTURING. *DRAW near to me. You are mine.*

Thankful for today, coolness, peacefulness, feeling filled with your LOVE.

Amen

May 18

$*\ *\ *$

AWAKENED LAST NIGHT, GRACE HAD noticed the part of the chair that was unpainted, I had painted a chair for her dressing table and she picked out the flaw. I was flooded with reminders of not being good enough in my life. The chair was the trigger.

I'm letting it go today. I am God's and He finds me good enough! He made me complete, whole and full of love and joy, humility and kindness. He loves me more than I can imagine loving my own children and for me, this is unimaginable. Being accepted by the Most High God is enough for me. Thank you for bringing my thoughts of "not good enough" to light so that I can completely give them up, release them to you. Thank you for taking them from me, this illusion that has affected me since I can remember. I, just like anyone else, just wants to be free of myself, the self-made up of everybody else in my life who was wounded, my wounded self.

Freedom is mine! I just need to claim it and never let it go. I WILL! I will do what is necessary to lie in it! Freedom through Christ, I'm drawing nearer to you O Lord. Amen

Galatians 5; 1

May 19

✳ ✳ ✳

NO LOOKING BACK, FRESH START. "remember no longer their sins or your own." *Throw away all that is un-important, all boundaries, past imperfections and failures. Press on.*

II Corinthians 12 77-10

May 20

∗ ∗ ∗

Do I see truth? Am I naïve? Use me O Lord in the way you see fit, your will be done.

Seeking to know you more, trusting, relinquishing, and letting go.

Thank you for training me and loving me and opening my heart and mind to your greatness, your majesty. God is great and I am enough in His eyes, in His arms. I am His and this is ALL that matters. Not my will but thine be done O Lord.

Amen

May 21

* * *

KEEP YOUR EYE ON THE prize, not on difficulties. Focus on how far I've come not how far I have to go.

God's key gifts power and LOVE." My presence will go with you wherever you go and I will give you rest."

Open our eyes O lord to see the bigger picture.

May 22

* * *

I AM A TEMPLE OF the Holy Spirit! Walking into freedom, one step at time towards presence, consciousness, and awareness.

I am who I AM! I am with you.

When you lead, I will follow. Thank you O Lord.

Amen

May 23

✳ ✳ ✳

WORSHIP, TRUST AND GIVE THANKS! Thank you O Lord. Amen

May 24

* * *

YOUR PRESENCE IS WITH US, you are with us. God with us. We cannot hide from your spirit O Lord and for this I am thankful.

May 25

* * *

I AM WEAK BUT YOU O Lord are strong.

It is because of my weakness that I know you better, more intimately. You have allowed me to get an understanding of seeing you more clearly because I failed myself.

You move mountains and all that's required of me is faith of a mustard seed? Because once I begin to put my faith in you it can't help but grow. Your wonders abound, my eyes are open, and I'm awake and alive! I see you, I sense your presence. You are the great I AM. Your will be done. Amen

May 26

* * *

THANK YOU FOR MY WEAKNESSES. It's through them and because of them that I seek your face because I am weak but you O Lord are my strength, my rock, my everything! Thank you for refreshing and renewing my mind. Keep me close, no matter what it takes.

May 27

* * *

ABIDE IN ME, ABIDE IN me. I will give you shelter, I will give you rest.

May 28

* * *

SURRENDER SELF; BE QUIET; BE still; hear my voice? I am with you every second, my divine love covering you completely. Listen and pay attention, be watchful and I will show you the way. My right hand guiding your every step, keep close to me. Get higher, continually seeking, making progress toward my light, my love towards ME.

May 29

* * *

WE LOVE BECAUSE HE FIRST loved us. God IS love IS God. He is
spirit and light, holy and powerful, faithful and true and just.

1 John 3; 16
1 John 12
1 John 4; 7

May 30

* * *

SUNDAY MORNING, I'M WILLING, AWAKE and searching. I have a knowing that God is in complete control and that He is the ultimate comforter and provider, the source from which we originate and to which we will go home to, in the heavens. Eternity, our human minds cannot begin to imagine what awaits us there, but I do know that we see glimpses of it here on earth everyday, we just have to be paying attention.

Goodness and Light:

"You may trod me in the very dirt but still like dust I will rise."
Maya Angelou

May 31ˢᵗ

✳ ✳ ✳

Goodness and Light:

Poetry has resonated with me since I was a little girl, The Real Mother Goose, Robert Louis Stephenson, Robert Frost and many others. When I lost Will, I made sure a poem was read at his burial. I searched until I found the perfect one, "A Good Boy," by Robert Louis Stephenson. Poetry touches me in the deepest recesses of my soul and I believe this is where it comes from to its authors.

＊ ＊ ＊

A Good Boy
I woke before the morning,
I was happy all the day,
I never said an ugly word, but smiled and stuck to play.
And now at last the sun is going down behind the wood,
And I am very happy, for I know that I've been good.
My bed is waiting cool and fresh, with linen smooth and fair,
And I must be off to sleepsin-by, and not forget my prayer.
I know that, till to-morrow I shall see the sun arise,
No ugly dream shall fright my mind, no ugly sight my eyes.
But slumber hold me tightly till I waken in the dawn,
And hear the thrushes singing in the lilacs round the lawn.

Write about it

Write about it

June 1

* * *

Goodness and Light:

I exist as I am, that is enough.
If no other in the world be aware, I sit content,
And if each and all be aware, I sit content.
One world is aware, and by far the largest to me,
And that is myself.
And whether I come to my own today or in ten thousand
Or ten million years,
I can cheerfully take it now, or with equal cheerfulness,
I can wait.

Passage from Walt Whitman's *"Leaves of Grass"*

June 2

* * *

REMAIN IN HIM, THE GIVER of life; nourished by the Vine, strengthened by His truth, his promise for overflowing, abundant life. We are becoming one with Him, He who remains the same yesterday, today and forever.

Philippians 4; 4

June 3

* * *

WITH GOD ALL THINGS ARE possible. He will refresh our minds and renew our souls and bring us back unto a childlike faith, by taking away all of the hurt and replacing it with His healing. All he asks of us is to trust and be still.

Mathew 19; 26

June 4

✳ ✳ ✳

I DON'T HAVE TO DO anything to receive the love of God. He loves me because He made me and I am His. I can rest and feel safe under the perfect protection of the divine.

Ephesians 2; 8

June 5

✳ ✳ ✳

IN QUIET STILLNESS YOU WILL find me. Here and now, the present. You will be given strength for today. All that is required is faith in me; trust in me, nothing else. Rest and relax in the ONE who breathed the very life into you, the ONE whose image you are beautifully and wonderfully made.

Not my will but thine be done, O Lord. Amen

Genesis 2; 7

June 6

* * *

HOW MANY TIMES WILL YOU say, "I'm sorry."? It's ok, you are forgiven, I accept you right where you are, now rest in that knowing, sense our connection, my presence. You can trust in me, I will never leave your side; it is you that walks away from me. If you can only grasp the power you have through me. You are weak but I am strong. I will never leave you or forsake you.

II Corinthians 12; 10
Deuteronomy 31; 8

June 7

* * *

THANK YOU LORD FOR COVERING me, for loving me through, for sustaining me.

Amen

Psalm 107; 1

June 8

* * *

SURRENDERING SELF WITH FORGIVENESS AND recognition, realization that I am not in control nor do I want to be. Knowing the hugeness of God and His power and that His good and perfect will is the reason for my life. He made me, He is my father, and He loves me completely. He will never disappoint me. He is all knowing, all-powerful and I am His child. I need only to surrender self, release control and rest in Him. Receive his gifts, one of which is peace of mind, for humans, the gift of all gifts.

Romans 12; 2

June 9

✳ ✳ ✳

To grow in relationship with God, to mature and be more like our Creator, we must spend time with Him, acknowledging He IS who He IS. Do not become distracted by things that are meaningless. Stay present minded, this awareness will save you. His Will, WILL be laid out before you.

June 10

* * *

I AM EMPOWERED BY GOD. I am thankful that I know that each second is a gift given me by God. His will be done, your will be done.

June 11

***

WE ARE GIVEN MANY CHANCES in our lives to choose God. Once chosen, the opportunity to get to know him and be intimately present with Him becomes another choice. Being completely alone with no one to talk to, no one to share my troubles with, and no one to lean on or depend on has become my salvation. I am so thankful I was put in this place of utter loneliness because it was from this place that I was found by you. It was from this place that I received and recognized you O Lord, your spirit and a knowing that you are with me constantly, to the ends of the earth. I am not lonely anymore, for you are with me, always. God with us, God with me.

June 12

* * *

Experience His majesty, his splendor His peace and joy. Dwell with him.

I Corinthians 3; 16

Goodness and Light:

To dwell means to make your home in, to exist in a given place or state. Dwell with God.

June 13

✳ ✳ ✳

I SURRENDER ALL, AND THEN continually seek His Will, resting in His sovereignty. In so doing, I am free from fear, free to give thanks. Resting quietly in His presence covered in LIGHT and LOVE.

June 14

* * *

I WANT TO KNOW YOU more. I want to understand my reason for being, my purpose, your will for my life. Thank you for continually opening my heart and my mind, my soul, my eyes to see you.

June 15

* * *

I TRUST IN YOU O Lord. I know that you love me completely. Help me to be free, help me to be me.

Light lives in a soul surrendered.

June 16

∗ ∗ ∗

STANDING ON THE OUTSIDE OF a glass looking in, watching, longing to be included, accepted and loved just for who I am, for me.

Rest and relax knowing God has us covered completely and will provide all that's needed each second. Trust in God's promises, not my feelings. Live and let live.

June 17

* * *

YOU ARE HERE O LORD; it is your presence I seek. Your presence is where I wish to rest and lay my head. Fill me with your goodness with your love with your light. Your will be done. I surrender myself to you mind, body and soul. You O Lord promise to make me and mold me, to protect and keep me always and forevermore.

Amen

June 18

* * *

WE ARE WORKS OF ART, planned and purposed by God.

Your will be done.

June 19

✳ ✳ ✳

THERE'S NO PRESSURE WHEN WE understand and recognize that we are not in control nor do we want to be. We have a God, our Father our Shepherd who knows ALL who sees ALL, who works for our good. The gift lies in the understanding, a knowing, and an acceptance that we are not in control. To surrender ALL to surrender self completely to this knowing shows ultimate strength, not weakness. This brings a flood of peace that cannot be described. The kicker is that this happens usually when we are at our weakest, this step of faith occurs when we give up our will for that of God, our faith in the unseen has to be grown and nurtured and nourished in order for this miracle to occur.

June 20

✳ ✳ ✳

ONE STEP AT A TIME, focus my mind on you, trusting, knowing you have laid out my steps before me and are holding me fast, my right hand in yours. Joyfully I walk with thee, I pray thy will be done. Thank you for this day, a gift to live, to be free to experience LIFE. Thank you for your forgiveness and enabling us to forgive. I will see you today in everything.

June 21

*** * * *

TO BE GOD-CENTERED IS FEELING, exuding, being ONE through love energy, complete surrender, complete acceptance in totality. ONE merged in and through LOVE, seeking the divine.

June 22

* * *

DWELL WITH GOD, PRAYING HIS will be done. Spirit will flow through me as a channel reaching into the lives of others. Dwell in HIM. For it is through Him, because of Him, in HIM, I LIVE and move and have my being.

June 23

* * *

FORGIVE THE PAST, LEARN THE lesson, remember the good and press on, move forward.

June 24

* * *

FOCUS ENTIRELY ON CHRIST; HIS presence and I will be completely covered with LOVE and peace. Relaxing in His presence, he will mold me and make me, refresh and renew my very soul. Stillness, be still and know that God's presence is here waiting for us to see.

June 25

* * *

THE COLORS OF HEAVEN, GOD the artist; surrender all to him. A stone in a mosaic fits perfectly in His time in the pattern he created, the artist and his masterpiece.

Everlasting to everlasting.

Amen

June 26

∗ ∗ ∗

PEACE BE STILL. THANK YOU Lord for this day our daily bread. Thank you for your forgiveness, help us to forgive others in the same way you forgave us. Thank you for your love and your light for it is through you "we live and move and have our being." Thy will be done. My belief in you, our belief in you gives us life everlasting.

Praise you O Lord.

Amen and Amen

June 27

* * *

LORD THANK YOU FOR YOUR protection, healing, provision, sovereignty, LOVE and assurance. Thank you, Thank you, Thank you O Lord! You are my everything!

Amen and Amen

June 28

* * *

I AM THANKFUL FOR GRACE, for healing through your mighty power. I am thankful for Emily Drew and for Grace Anne. I am thankful for health and well-being, your Holy Spirit, surrender, truth, strength and connection.

Your will be done.

Amen

June 29

* * *

TODAY IS THE ONLY THING that matters and this moment has already passed.

Set my mind on you O Lord. Your will I continue to seek. Not my will but thine O Lord. Not my will but thine be done.

Amen

June 30

* * *

GOD IS IN CONTROL so I can rest and enjoy my days. I spent a lot of time alone in my life and I consider it a blessing now. I love others more than they will ever know or believe. My girls are the reason I want to be the best that I can be. I tend to gravitate towards the wallflowers in a crowd. I enjoy quiet places and listening to soulful music. I love to cook and have watched cooking shows since I can remember. I can ride a unicycle. I can stand on my head. I love the beach, the mountains and the skies because they remind me of how very small I am in comparison to what God has created. I love the outdoors, just being one with nature, pretending I'm in a painting, a masterpiece created by God. I have a child-like imagination. I love children, children's books, musicals and tapping into my child-like self. I like to read as long as I'm learning something from it. I'm in awe of artists, musicians, dancers, writers, those gifted and living purposefully. I believe that all that we need is in our own backyard. I'm an eternal optimist. I don't like being the center of attention. I would rather observe conversation than be involved in it. The biggest obstacle I've overcome in my life is not feeling good enough. Simplicity is the hidden treasure for which we all are searching, it can't be bought and once lost, is hard to find again. What we all are longing for is connection, one with spirit one with creation, oneness.

Write about it

Write about it

July 1

* * *

THANK YOU FOR THIS BEAUTIFUL morning. Thank you for a good night's rest, for a strong mind and body, for a soul seeking you all day long.

Everlasting to everlasting. Amen

Opening; accepting; relaxing. Seeking…

July 2

* * *

BEAUTY LIES BEFORE US EVERY day every second beckoning our attention, waiting patiently for us to open our eyes and see, all day long and into the night.

July 3

* * *

THROUGH THE EYES OF A child we see you. Pleasing you, accepting your love, trusting, and walking, always thankful despite our circumstances.

July 4

* * *

GOD YOU ARE WITH US, ever-present, all knowing, omniscient. We cannot hide from the LOVE of God.

July 5

FEELING SAD BUT SEARCHING, SEEKING truth, love and light despite what's going on. Keep me, sustain me, allow me to sense your presence by opening my eyes, my heart to know how high and deep and wide is your love.

July 6

* * *

FILL UP WITH THANKFULNESS. CONTINUE building a firm foundation of gratitude by remembering nothing can separate us from the love of God. Receive His peace as I lay me down to sleep with a lullaby of love singing softly, softly as I drift off to sleep in the safety of your arms.

July 7

* * *

A LOT TO LEARN, I take full responsibility, I'm asking for clarity and freedom from past hurts and failures. Thank you O Lord for your love, help me to bathe in it today, to experience your love in the midst of conflicted emotion. Help me to completely relinquish control and to bathe in the light of your love.

Amen

July 8

* * *

"COME NEAR TO ME AND I will give you rest." "Draw near to me and I will draw near to you." Fill up with joy and peace; yours for the taking grounded in thankfulness, never ceasing, making us humble, resting in His love, his arms. "Come near to me and I will come near to you" and fill you to overflowing with living water, my joy and my peace. Our hope is in you O Lord all day long. Your will be done.

Amen

July 9

* * *

WALK WITH ME; I AM your protector, mind, body and soul. You can count on me; I will never leave you nor forsake you. I am the great I AM.

July 10

* * *

EXPAND YOUR VISION; SEE THE world as I see it. Remember the sky has no limit, the seas, the mountains, my LOVE is infinite, greater than any of these, and your mind cannot grasp it. Meditate to be close to me, stay awake and aware, and be present with me. I am in the NOW, stay with me, seek me, see me in all things, I am here.

July 11

✳ ✳ ✳

THE BEAUTY OF CHARACTER AND spirit, beauty of love and life, abundant life found in each of us, placed here by God. One body made in his image with peaceful hearts. Be thankful for the Lord is good, his love endures forever and ever from ever-lasting to everlasting.

Amen

July 12

* * *

WE ARE MADE IN THE likeness of God, in his image. I am to trust him in all circumstances always giving thanks always giving praise, knowing that he is with me, no doubting. He has promised abundant life, beautiful and peaceful LIFE. Give thanks to the lord for he is GOOD his love endures forever.

July 13

* * *

I REMAIN THANKFUL LORD, HERE with you, relaxing in you, blending together, so exquisite, so intricately woven, centered, connected, radiantly beaming.

One with you Lord. ONE.

July 14

* * *

BUILDING A FOUNDATION THAT'S IMMOVABLE, stayed in thankfulness, strengthened by trusting and knowing that you will provide what is necessary in order for us to grow and bloom and flourish. We are rooted and established in LOVE.

July 15

∗ ∗ ∗

LINKING UP WITH SPIRIT, CONNECTING one to the other, seeking the divine through prayer, watchfulness, present mindedness, remaining thankful for ALL.

July 16

* * *

I AM WORTHY. I AM peace. I am forgiveness. I am love. I am compassion. I am a child of the Most High God. I am his beloved.

Thanks be to God.

July 17

∗ ∗ ∗

EVER PRESENT, ALL KNOWING, ALL encompassing, everlasting, God, you are mighty you are strong you are indefinable. Praise and honor and glory to God!

July 18

* * *

I PRAY TO BE CLOSER with thee. Even though I cannot see you, I love you. I believe in your power and strength and continually pray a closer walk with thee.

July 19

I AM WITH YOU AND I will watch over you wherever you go. Surely God is in this place, and He IS! O Lord I am so thankful for thee. When will we understand that the best you have to offer is waiting for us if we will just learn to receive it? Letting go of self and our own desires and letting you take the reigns, allowing you to determine our steps, our words our thoughts our deeds. Letting go is such a miracle, knowing that you've got us, we can trust you completely, we need not fear, for you O Lord, are Mighty to save!

July 20

* * *

JOY IN TOTAL SECURITY AS we take refuge in the Lord and His perfect Will for our lives is laid out before us. This requires our total involvement and commitment, our whole being, our DEVOTION.

July 21

* * *

I AM YOURS COMPLETELY, MAKE me and mold me into your complete and perfect Will. I bow down in your presence, lest I stray, be quick to bring me back to you, into your everlasting arms into the safety of your love. Amen

July 22

I am strong because of God. He is my strength.
I am beautiful because of the Lord. I am his child.
I am courageous because He is with me.
I love because he loves me.
I am willing because I follow him.
I am because he IS the great I AM.

July 23

* * *

I PRAY BLESSINGS UPON THOSE who are weary, who are sad who are hurting. Lift them out of themselves and into your light, a light that never ceases to shine even what we can't see past the darkness you are here, waiting, watching. Reach out, lift your hands to the sky, surrender your pain and He will replace it with his love.

July 24

∗ ∗ ∗

I SEE YOU LORD, ALL day long. I awaken giving thanks for life looking forward to my day, resting in the peace you promise when our focus is on your presence. I see you in the eyes of others and recognize connection, sameness, despite our physical bodies our spirits are one. I see you all day long and sense your presence even though I cannot see you, you are invisible to the eye but you are here, among us. I know that you are here, a mighty force more powerful than the waves of the sea, quiet stillness is where you abide, I must continue seeking to know you more in the stillness of my mind.

I honor you in stillness and I seek you all day long. I see you even though I cannot. I see you and I feel your presence, your love.

July 25

* * *

LOOK UP AND AWAY, BE strong, be thankful, be courageous. I AM the great I AM your father, your savior your hope. Rest in me.

July 26

* * *

MIRACLES UNFOLDING BEFORE MY VERY eyes, your love is better than life itself, your unfailing love. Love casts out all fear. I am thankful, searching, prayerful, humbled.

July 27

✳ ✳ ✳

CLOSING MY EYES TO HONOR thee, to be closer to thee, knowing that I am never alone. I am beyond thankful for this knowing, for your love, an unending and indefinable love. I am thankful for the gift of imagination that makes belief in the unseen real.

July 28

∗ ∗ ∗

A CLOSER WALK WITH THEE I pray. Rejoice! Sing praises! Hallelujah to our King. He IS the light of the world!

Psalm 95; 1-5

July 29

* * *

THANKFUL O LORD THAT YOU have led me to receive what you have been offering to us every single day, your peace, your love, your light.

Psalm 90; 2

"Humility like darkness reveals the heavenly lights."

Henry David Thoreau

July 30

* * *

It's TIME TO LIVE MY purpose to start standing up and living my truth, God's Will for my life! I am weak but you O Lord are strong! Not my will but thine be done!

July 31

* * *

BUILD NOW ON A FIRM foundation. I am your rock, I shall not move, I shall remain steadfast and firm. Trust and place full faith in this: I will not move. Experience victory NOW.

Thanks be to God! Amen

Write about it

_____

_____

_____

_____

_____

_____

_____

_____

_____

_____

_____

_____

_____

_____

_____

_____

_____

_____

_____

_____

_____

_____

_____

_____

_____

_____

_____

_____

Write about it

August 1

∗ ∗ ∗

OUR LORD THOU ART HERE, let us feel thy nearness.

Psalm 89; 15

Blessed are those who have learned to acclaim you who walk in the light of your presence O Lord.

August 2

∗ ∗ ∗

To FLOURISH, TO HAVE PERFECT peace requires a steadfast mind. You will keep in perfect peace him whose mind is steadfast on you.

Love and Light:

I can choose perfect peace? And all that is required is trusting God, the ONE who created the world and all that is in it? The One who has no beginning and no end? The ONE who is eternal and the very foundation of the world?

August 3

* * *

WE ARE WORKS OF ART fashioned in the likeness of God, our Father. In order for us to flourish, to thrive we are to remain in Him, connected. We can do this by spending a little time, every day, seeking Him, reading His word dwelling on His promises, believing and receiving His gifts, one of which is the gift of LIFE and remaining thankful. Dwell on goodness. God is good. Dwell on love, God IS love.

Ephesians 2; 10
1 John 4 7-8

August 4

GOD IN US. GOD WITH us. God through us. We are powerful because of Him. "I can do all things through Christ who strengthens me." Without God I am nothing with God I am everything. God centered, God focused, God is everything and everywhere. I rest in your peace, given me freely because I trust in you.

Thanks be to God! Amen

August 5

* * *

GOD IS ON THE THRONE. I am thankful for the ability to dream, to pray, to hope, to be thankful.

August 6

* * *

HELP ME TO LOVE AND be loved. Help me to give and to receive. My focus is on your Will and your word, one day at a time. Always remembering, "Today is the day that the Lord hath made, Let us rejoice and be glad in it."

August 7

✳ ✳ ✳

I AM DEVOTED TO YOU. I will lavish you with love, with my peace. Trust in me, with a child-like trust, I will not disappoint you. "Peace I leave with you; my peace I give you. I do not give to you as the world gives. Do not let your hearts be troubled and do not be afraid."

John 14; 27

August 8

* * *

PRAY AND READ MY BIBLE, train and discipline myself, this is my responsibility so that God can use me for His purposes. Thy will be done. Stay awake! Trust in the Lord, be patient and he will strengthen you. He will see you through.

Thanks be to God! Amen

August 9

✳ ✳ ✳

I AM THE EVER PRESENT God. Hope is a gift given and received through spirit connection. Trust, be still, and be present with me. I will guide your every step.

My trust is in you all day long.

Thankful for relationship with God for it is through Him I LIVE and MOVE and have my being. Because of you I have life and for this I am thankful. "Give thanks to the Lord for he is good his love endures forever…"

Psalm 107; 1

August 10

* * *

DWELL ON MY PROMISES, SEEK my face, rest in my arms, I will guide you through.

Thank you for today, for the beauty that surrounds us. For your protection as we go from here to there, for the love we share. Thank you for presence of mind, your light, and your love. Strengthen us O Lord to serve you well, to seek out your Will and the courage to take action necessary to fulfill it.

Thanks be to God! Amen

August 11

* * *

THANK YOU LORD FOR HELPING me, for teaching me to listen. *Pour out your requests; be thankful for answers to prayers. Continually communicate with me, focus on ME and my abiding presence. "My presence will go with you and I will give you rest."*

Exodus 33; 14

August 12

* * *

I SAW BRIGHT BEAUTIFUL WINGS standing out among the dry leaves. I can't help but bend down and pick you up, your battered wings still full of color, catching my eye. I picture you flying in the springtime, making me smile, and giving me joy. I look forward to seeing you flit and float and FLY, bursting with LIFE! Not too long from now, not too long from now. Keep catching our eyes beautiful butterflies, keep our eyes on you because you know something more than we, as we follow you until you seem to disappear, not too long from now, not too long from now.

August 13

* * *

THE PRESENT, RIGHT NOW, IS where I will find you and is where I wish to be. Thank you Lord for opening my eyes to this truth. Keep me present, in your presence, seeking, watching, and paying attention to your guidance, your Will. Praying for all to stop and pay attention. Praying for surrender to your Will and your way. I trust in you with my whole being with all that I am.

August 14

∗ ∗ ∗

I GIVE YOU MY ALL for you are my everything. Thank you Lord, I pray to bathe in your joy and to remain close to you.

August 15

$*\ *\ *$

GOD WITH US. *"I AM **with you.**"*

August 16

* * *

ALL IS WELL, FOCUS ON ME. Surrender self.

I'm all in.

Thanks be to God.

August 17

* * *

ILLUMINATE OUR MINDS SO THAT we can continue to bloom and flourish in your love, strengthened and whole, just being, just thankful, shining forth your light.

August 18

* * *

THANK YOU LORD FOR YOUR LOVE, holding us close, bathing us in your light. I receive it today. I pray to be present with you, to flourish among the beauty of the universe, which you created for us to live and to thrive in.

My trust is in you all day long.

August 19

✳ ✳ ✳

THANKS BE TO GOD FOR you O Lord are good. Joy filled, today and everyday. I pray for your joy, your love, to fill us to overflowing because you are with us. God with us and this is ALL that matters.

August 20

* * *

JOY IS A GIFT AND we must learn to receive it. Trust in God and He will make our paths straight and continually brighten our days with the light of His love.

August 21

* * *

THY WILL BE DONE. LIMITLESS, unending, everlasting, infinite, unceasing, human words used to describe a God who is indescribable, the human mind cannot fathom can never fully understand the power of Almighty God.

God is ALL, He is everything.

"Be still and know that I am God."

August 22

I AM NOT I, I am His and He lives in me and through me directing my steps, lighting the way. Rejoice in the lord, Rejoice! Sing joy to the Lord for He is good, His love endures forever!

August 23

* * *

WHAT I AM WILLING TO give, I will receive.

I am your ever-present help. Lean on me, I will not disappoint; I am with you always, to the ends of the earth and beyond. I am ALL. I am everything, lean on me and I will show you the way.

August 24

∗ ∗ ∗

COME TO ME. SURRENDER ALL to ME, Give ALL to ME and you will receive ALL. "I AM ALL." "I am everything." Come unto me, rest in me. "I AM the great I AM.

Love and Light:

If I were a flower I would be a tulip always bending towards the light, delicate, pristine, fragile and lovely.

August 25

∗ ∗ ∗

He fills me up to overflowing everyday all day long! Focus on Him! He will direct our steps every second of every day. Lord you are my strength and my healer, thank you for joy, peace and connection.

August 26

* * *

GUARD OUR HEARTS AND MINDS O Lord. May we constantly, unceasingly dwell on you and your promises of peace? Thank you Lord for your love, your light. Thank you O Lord for Life. We are nothing without you. God with us.

August 27

* * *

PEACE THAT SURPASSES ALL UNDERSTANDING, spirit connection one to the other, and courage to live in truth. Get higher; move closer to the most powerful God, the creator of the Universe.

August 28

* * *

YOU ARE WITH ME, WITH us. Your hold me by my right hand. If I focus on you, remain in you, you will make my paths straight, you will shine your light amid the darkness. I am a child of God, your child, therefore I am enough.

August 29

✳ ✳ ✳

BECAUSE I AM A CHILD of God, I am enough! He will make me shine, He will continually renew and refresh my spirit and make me more like Him. Rest in Him, rely on Him. God with us. You are with us. Thank you Lord, Praise you, love you. Amen

Love and Light:

When my time comes around, I will be found by you and I can just be me, the ME you created me to BE!

August 30

∗ ∗ ∗

ENVISION WHAT I WISH TO be, the life I wish to live. Thankful for your love, opening my mind, sharing of your vision and your love and your power, your Will.

Thank you Lord.

August 31

✳ ✳ ✳

I PRAY TO LEARN TO receive your grace and your love, knowing that I am made in your likeness and that I am a child of the Most High God. I pray for your guidance and protection for my loved ones and myself and for mankind. I pray thankfulness for this day to live and learn and be the person you meant for me to be. Your Will, your good and perfect Will be done.

Write about it

Write about it

September 1

THANK YOU LORD FOR YOU are Great, our protector, our redeemer. Thank you for your grace freely given, for your love for your everlasting love. I am thankful.

September 2

I CAN DO ALL THINGS through Christ who strengthens me. *Fix your eyes on me, all day long, trust and be thankful.*

September 3

I will be found.

Trust in me, I will lead you, guide you continually. Doubts are not of God. Fear is not of God. Trust completely in Him. God loves us, tenderly loves us. Trust in his love, the only one who can love us perfectly.

Replace your fears with my promises, my peace, no doubting.

Jesus died to save us from darkness, sin, doubt and worry. Accept His love, believe and receive His LOVE.

September 4

GUARD YOURSELVES AGAINST SELF-PITY BY focusing on God and thanking him, praising him, loving him. Be still in the knowledge of God's love everlasting.

September 5

* * *

BE DEVOTED. I AM IN God, as God is in me.

Lift up your hands to the heavens as high as they can stretch! Breathe in and feel the radiance of God's love infiltrating every pore of my body from my fingertips to my toes. Filling up with thankfulness and praise, joy and love for the ONE who made me. Breathe in again and be present with Him.

September 6

* * *

I am with you.

THANK YOU LORD THAT YOU are everywhere and everything. Keep my mind focused on your miracles beginning with the miracle of life and health and the ability to connect through love and acceptance, one to the other.

September 7

* * *

PLEASING GOD IS ALL THAT matters. Steadily, walking uphill, all the way with God at my side. Seeking him in stillness and throughout my day, focusing on Him. God with us.

"I am with you, always to the very end of the age."

September 8

* * *

I AM WHAT I AM. My goal is to completely relinquish control and live an exemplary life with the fullness of God devouring my mind, body and spirit.

September 9

* * *

LIVING EACH DAY WITH FULLNESS of joy that can only come from God. Thankful and prayerful, seeing through the lenses of our creator, a living artwork surrounded by endless shades of color from the skies to the depths of the earth on which we stand. Our world, a work of art, continually moving, always in motion, ever changing, swirling with miracles. Eternity awaits us, forever and ever, there is no end.

September 10

* * *

DIVINE LOVE, UNCHANGING, CONSTANT FROM the source, God ever-lasting. Thank you O Lord. God with us.

"I am with you" forever, to the very end of the age, eternally yours. I am the source of ALL, the fruit of the spirit abide in me. I am here, a constant companion for all who seek my name. "Seek me and you will find me when you seek me with all of your heart I will be found by you, says the Lord.

September 11

PRAISE YOU O LORD FOR your unending LOVE. May we be more like you, seeking and searching everyday to find you, to see you in all things good and seemingly bad? You are everything and I love you. Thank you for today to live to explore to BE. One with you O Lord, this is our prayer.

September 12

∗ ∗ ∗

Because you are my help
I sing in the shadow of your wings
My soul clings to you; your right hand upholds me.

Psalm 63; 7-8

September 13

* * *

I HONOR YOU O LORD and I am thankful.

The tree, her name is LO.

Small yet strong, ready to take root in soil fertilized with love, hope and joy. Watered with care, knowing, sureness of a long journey ahead. Symbolizing life, renewal.

The tree, it's foundation assuring growth and maturity, ready to take on and weather any storm, totally dependent on it's maker to give life and open and ready to receive it. Take root beautiful tree, flourish, be what you are meant to be, a tree.

September 14

∗ ∗ ∗

I AM PERFECT, YOUR CREATION, made in your likeness. I am made to love and be loved, to teach as I am taught, to give what I am given.

"Rest in me, you are my forever child, my offspring, forever connected, never separated. I am your protector, your father "I am with you always to the very ends of the earth, rest in me."

September 15

✳ ✳ ✳

FOCUS ON LOVE, HOLDING THE right hand of God our Father, secure, free to live, to experience the abundance that can only be found through the love of our redeemer, our creator. Let go and see goodness, let go and see God. Let go and live, freedom awaits us.

September 16

$* * *$

I'M LEARNING TO RECEIVE; I'M learning to give. I'm learning that to give IS to receive.

Love and Light

"Believe it and you will see it." Wayne Dyer

September 17

✳ ✳ ✳

I'M FEELING MORE AND MORE like me.

Thank you Lord for opening my eyes to see you more clearly, your words your promises are no longer dim and hard to discern they are shining like the light at the end of a storm and are covered in colors like a rainbow signifying the storm has passed and we can rest in this knowing.

I remember reading your word and being frustrated because it was so foreign, so hard to understand. But now, your words I know are truth and the meaning goes so deep we cannot begin to understand it's full meaning. I am so thankful that my search is over at least for the knowing that you are real, that your promises are true that the more we surrender to self the more the veil will be lifted and the closer we will come to you, the ultimate source of LOVE, my father, my Lord.

September 18

✳ ✳ ✳

I AM YOUR SANCTUARY. YOUR light, your love shining forth even in the darkness if you choose to see, to open your eyes, your hearts, your minds. To believe I am with you always even though you cannot see me, this is faith believing in the unseen, the light in the darkness, that goodness always overcomes evil, where I long for you to dwell. "I am here."

You are with us because your word says you "will never leave us nor forsake us" and I know this is truth and I choose to dwell in your light, your love, your presence O Lord.

"I am with you always to the very end of the age."

September 19

* * *

TRUST IS THE SUM OF it ALL. O Lord Almighty blessed is the man who trusts in you. Your Will be done on earth as it is in heaven.

September 20

MY TRUST IS IN YOU all day long and into the night, my trust is in you. Thank you for today, may I live in a way that is pleasing to you. This is the sum of it all. You are ALL.

September 21

* * *

THANK YOU LORD FOR TODAY, for life, for love. Thank you for continually opening our eyes through whatever means possible so that we can see you more clearly.

Help me to remember that you orchestrate my life, everyday, every second and that if I'm paying attention, your plans for me, your Will for my life will be laid out plain before me. Trust in the Lord.

September 22

✳ ✳ ✳

HIGHER LOVE. I FEEL MYSELF soften, relax and exhale. I feel the breath of life flowing in and out of my body. I see, hear, smell, taste and touch because of you O Lord. Your light emanating all around us and shining forth. Can I see it? The sky is always blue if you can strengthen your gaze to see beyond the clouds." In your light we see light.

Psalm 36; 9

September 23

✳ ✳ ✳

IF WE BELIEVE THAT HEAVEN is real and that we will reunite with all of our loved ones one glorious day, what do we have to fear? And is fear an emotion that comes from a loving God? If we trust and have faith that God is "the beginning and the end" can't we live today relaxing in His strength, enjoying the abundance of the earth, expressing the fruits of the spirit; love, joy, peace, patience, kindness, goodness, gentleness and self control? Can we imagine that hard times are meant to teach us, to grow us, to move us towards a more god-centered mind and ultimately towards God?

We are to learn so that we can be taught and then teach others who are struggling like we were. If this were our last week on earth would we accept it and live it by loving the rest of our days or would we resist it and be angered and fight it? We are here on earth for one another. We are to love one another, we are equal in God's eyes and He loves us all the same. God with us.

September 24

✳ ✳ ✳

*"LET GO, I AM HERE." **Intimate knowledge of me is the very foundation of your faith.***

Letting go, surrendering self, knowing that there is a power source completely in control of the world, the universe and all that is in it. This knowing is what we strive for. A faith anchored by a KNOWING, knowledge, an intimacy with the ONE who is its CREATOR.

Love and Light

How often have I read? "Let go, I am here." I either believe it or I don't. If I believe "God with us" then I have nothing to fear. And since God works for the good of those who love him, then I know that letting go, surrendering self is what's best for me.

September 25

* * *

WATCHFUL, DISCIPLINED, SEEKING; WHEN I am feeling bothered or feeling hurt, it's usually because I've allowed Self/ego (edging God out) to creep in and overshadow spirit. Then I am quickly reminded that God is Sovereign, He is with me and His love shines forth so bright that darkness is no longer visible.

September 26

* * *

Be still in His presence.

"REST IN THE POWER OF my Spirit enveloped by my love, feel joy.

The best words I have to offer right now is to practice being still. We read, "Be still and know that I am God." *"Rest in my presence."*

Love and Light:

I know that the beginning of honoring God and being in his presence and understanding the power of his spirit begins with being still. Stillness allows us to discern God's voice apart from our own. The quieter we can become within ourselves, the closer we come to the Holy Spirit within us, God with us. It's impossible to hear God in the noise, so practice and learn to be still.

September 27

✳ ✳ ✳

A CHILD LOOKS TO ADULTS for acceptance, for love, for protection and security. A child knows that they need a leader to follow so that he can learn and grow and mature. What a responsibility growing up a child is!

Dear Lord, I pray that my children recognize that I am only human, but you are eternal and they are yours first and you O Lord will never disappoint them. You will hold them safe and secure in your everlasting arms. Thank you for the gift of our children, these beautiful, kind hearted children who have opened my eyes and heart to something bigger and more wondrous then myself.

"Give thanks to the Lord for He is Good his love endures forever."

September 28

***

LOVE THE LORD WITH A child-like wonder. Seek him knowing he will be found by you. Being sure, never doubting his love for you. Trusting in his promises, joy abounding, experiencing life to the full, knowing that when we are hurting, he is with us, he will make it better and we will be ok. Have faith like a child's, unshakeable, tender, trusting, pure.

September 29

* * *

To surrender is not weakness, it is recognition and knowing that we are not in control of our lives, it's an understanding that there's a force, a power that we can't begin to reckon with. I am weak but He is strong. It's giving in, not relying on our own strength but resting and relaxing and trusting in our creators.

He who made the heavens and the earth, He who made us. Just the magnitude of this understanding should induce surrender and then knowing that He is on our side, not an enemy but our ally! He longs to take complete care of us if we will just allow Him. Surrender is ultimate freedom through Christ, freedom is serenity, and serenity is love.

September 30

THE NOW, THIS MOMENT, WHICH has already passed into another, the awareness of it, time passing, allows me to be free, at peace, accepting what is, with no judgment. I am ONE with all of life and can flow with its pulse with no effort except focus on the ease of my breathing and acceptance of what is, whether my perception is good or bad.

Write about it

Write about it

October 1

* * *

HELP US TO UNDERSTAND THAT you are with us always. It is us that neglect to acknowledge it. It is us that walk away.

Just thank him today for Life, a simple thank you will do. Talk to God as if you're talking to a friend or loved one. Throughout the day we thank you for eyes to see, for ears to hear for hands to touch. Thank you that we can taste and smell the goodness and bounty of the season at hand. Thank you for our bodies and healing our wounds our illnesses. Just thank you for everything!

October 2

✳ ✳ ✳

THANK YOU LORD FOR TODAY, help us to walk through it with you in the forefront of our minds, seeking thankfulness, showing love exuding your light. I pray that we can learn to love ourselves in the same way that you love us, fully, unconditionally, always remembering that your son paid the ultimate price for our sin and that we are forgiven. No guilt, no shame, you love us ANYWAY.

Help us O Lord to love ourselves and in so doing be able to love one another.

October 3

* * *

I WALKED OUT THIS MORNING into the Wonderful Land of Oz equipped with a heart, a brain and courage to boot. No need for a yellow brick road or witches good or bad or a man named OZ. I have inside of me all of the power necessary to be who I am meant to be and I know the ONE who will guide me as long as I keep my focus on Him and don't allow a beautiful field of poppies to lead me astray.

October 4

∗ ∗ ∗

TODAY I AM THANKFUL; I have no right not to be at peace, even when the storm rages because your word says, You WILL calm the storm, and I believe your word. Your power is limitless and so is mine because you are within me! Recognition of this is a gift, your gift that allows us to enjoy our days that are gone as swiftly as sand through an hourglass. But our time with you eternal God, is forever.

October 5

* * *

THANK YOU TODAY FOR LIFE, for waking me during the storm to an understanding that I am LOVE. Thank you that I believe it because through faith, I believe in you. Thank you that I can receive it as truth and KNOW that your are what I read "the light of the world."

October 6

✳ ✳ ✳

TREAT OTHERS AS I WISH to be treated; I am neither above nor below another human being, we are all just in different levels of consciousness but all are interconnected.

October 7

* * *

REALLY DELVING INTO THANKFULNESS, GOING deep wanting to be reminded that my body is a temple, marveling at it's functioning, it's energy. We awaken and thoughts are already screaming for attention. Who controls these thoughts? I take for granted and just expect that my body will do what it's always done, carry me from here to there with eyes that open and can see with ears to hear. Sometimes I forget to be thankful for my body. I read that it's a temple, a vessel that houses my soul and the Holy Spirit, the very spirit of God.

October 8

✳ ✳ ✳

Surrender signifies deeper wisdom, pure and utter devotion to God and all His majesty and sovereignty. It's hard to surrender self-reliance when life is easy and circumstances seem rosy and bright. No, it's during the storms the turmoil, the desolation, when a drink of water is all that is needed to refresh and sustain the weary soul, just a drink of cool, fresh water to give hope to a weary, worn down soul who only needs to surrender and trust and be saved.

October 9

* * *

COME AWAKE! THIS IS GOING to be a great day! Thank you Lord for guiding us through, eyes and hearts set on you, going about our day with the promises of fullness of hope, joy, peace and love. Our words and deeds and actions painting a picture of what life is, with you as our foundation, as the vine, as the maker of our souls.

Keep us humbled, grateful and whole so that we may grow into blossoms of hope strengthened by the force of your spirit.

October 10

* * *

WHEN WE GIVE WHAT ISN'T easy for us to give this is when our spirit is strengthened and opened up and we grow and change. This is truly a closer walk with thee. Thank you for the willingness, the courage, the boldness to listen and act, following your lead O Lord.

"But you remain the same and your years will never end."
Psalm 102; 27

October 11

***

AWAKENING TO WHOM WE REALLY are, loving spirits wanting to lend compassion and hope. Visiting the child within who is innocent and untouched by ugliness, she's here, within ready to be found and she WILL BE!

When I was a child I was pure and simple, seeing the world as a place of wonder, a place that would embrace me, nurture me and build me up with goodness, filling me with light and joy overflowing. I am her again building on a firm foundation that cannot be shaken by an unkind word or rolling of the eyes. This child, this girl, this woman is who God meant for her to be, she's a miracle and walking close to her Father, holding his hand knowing she cannot be disappointed or shamed ever again.

October 12

* * *

GETTING AN UNDERSTANDING OF FORGIVENESS and compassion, knowing that ugly words or anger only hurts me not the other. We must learn that anger, malice, gossip, unforgiveness and judgment is a reflection of our own character and hurts our own spirits first and then the spirit of another.

October 13

✳ ✳ ✳

THIS IS GOING TO BE a great day! Thank you Lord for guiding us through, eyes and hearts on you, going about our day with the promises of fullness of hope, faith, joy and peace. Our words and deeds and actions painting a picture of what life can be with you as the foundation, the fertile soil, the maker and creator of our souls. Keep us humbled, grateful, and whole so that we may grow into blossoms of hope strengthened by the force of your spirit blowing through us.

October 14

∗ ∗ ∗

WE READ TO LIVE IN gratitude, thankfulness in all circumstances, to discipline our minds, to be still, to love one another, to treat others as we ourselves wish to be treated, to judge not, to seek and we shall find, to love the Lord with all of our heart and soul, we read that God is the Alpha and Omega, everlasting, omnipotent, all powerful creator of heaven and earth and ALL that is in it. Surrender unto him; pray not my will but thine be done.

October 15

* * *

WE CAN AND SHOULD SENSE the presence of God everyday, all day, if we are paying attention and focused on goodness and thankfulness. It takes practice and action. Stopping our minds from incessant chatter about the past and the future and focusing on today, right now. God is providing what we need for each moment of life whether in joy or in sorrow. He provides for us, we can seek him on Sunday while we are at church and you will find him there, but we can also seek him today, right now and he is here. Open our eyes O Lord, to the light of your love.

October 16

WHERE WOULD I BE WITHOUT my possessions? Left, with just me, am I still worthy? Would others come to my aid? Would there be a way when everything seemed lost? To see that everything is within us, within our bodies, our shell our vessels are spirit, souls, temples, that cannot perish that cannot die. If we nurture it, feed it and water it with goodness and light, it will grow and be strengthened to know the truth of who it is and what it stands for.

Spirit alone is our strength, spirit alone is our comfort, and spirit connected to spirit is our destiny.

October 17

∗ ∗ ∗

THE BIBLE IS THE WORD of God, full of bounty, provision and sustenance for a soul that is weary and a soul that rejoices. The bible the very word of God when studied and steeped into our minds provides for a deeper and more fulfilling relationship with the master. The bible, the word of God is a gift that never stops giving until we believe, we know ALL and can dwell with our God and his grace until we come face to face with him.

October 18

* * *

RELEASE FEAR, FOLLOW ME. I go before you, trust in me. Focus on my promises and me and I will make your paths steady, rest and relax in my arms everlasting. Remain in my light, you cannot hide from me, you cannot hide from my love.

October 19

***

OPENING TO SEE, KEEPING FOCUSED on God and his word that assures us of victory no matter what we are going through. Thankfulness and gratitude keeps me close to the one who is our creator our maker our Father.

Be watchful and pull the weeds daily as they begin to come up and attempt to cover, to strangle the beauty of a plant that is thriving. If the weeds are not pulled and the plant pruned, soon we will look for the beautiful plant and weeds are all we will see.

October 20

* * *

I LOVE YOU LORD. I thank you for all that you are and all that you have done and will do to assure that we are cared for mind, body and soul. Thank you, Praise you, Love you.

October 21

* * *

US, PURE, KIND, COMPASSIONATE, LOVELY, tender, joyful, gentle peaceful; us, before the world, us, ONE with God, unblemished, unaffected, whole. May we be the children you created? Overflowing with your fruit spreading the seed of your love today and always. Amen

October 22

* * *

"For nothing is impossible with God."

I am love because God is love and I am made in His likeness. In His eyes I am a perfect creation. He loves me, I am enough in his eyes, we are enough.

October 23

LIFE IS A SYMPHONY; OUR senses give us all that is needed to fully experience the offerings of God. Awaken and sense the light of the morning, a choir of birds in tune beckoning a new day. Feeling our bodies refreshed and renewed, breathing in deeply to take in the crispness of the morning air, colors abounding, a feast for the eyes. Can you see it? Can you hear it?

I see, I hear, I taste, I smell, and I touch.

Thanks be to God.

October 24

* * *

SENSITIVE TO THE SPIRIT OF God used for his purposes, His will be done. It's not about me and I am so thankful to know this without a doubt. This knowledge, this freedom from hurt from offense, because God is the ONE I aim to please, His will is what I seek. Thankful that my eyes have been opened to see my humanness, my ego, that I can deal with it and put it away quickly by replacing it with God and his un-abounding, immeasurable LOVE that fills those holes with living water, overflowing with his majesty, his sovereignty, his power.

October 25

* * *

I MUST BE FULLY OPEN and awake, aware, present in order to absorb the living God. Pay attention today, seek his light and truth. Be thankful for life and the beautiful landscape provided to live it. Be in awe of your body, a temple for our spirits connecting us to our creator. Pay attention to your breathing, in and out, in and out without a thought. Be aware, be thankful, awaken to life today and absorb all of God's goodness, so abundant, so beautiful, and so alive.

October 26

IF THINGS AREN'T GOING THE way that brings us peace summon the courage to do something different. It's the first step that's always the hardest but it's stepping out of our comfort zones that help our faith to grow.

October 27

* * *

FILL US UP TO OVERFLOWING with your love, with your love. Open
our hearts and minds to receive all of your offerings and abundance of which we cannot begin to grasp. Your spirit, constant,
unchanging always pulling us in to you wanting us to trust
and rest, relax and know that your power is what propels the
universe.

October 28

* * *

SIMPLICITY OF LIFE, A LITTLE rest, a little sunshine, a little love given and received.

October 29

* * *

Just love me because I love you. Rest and know that you are protected. I know what you need, your provision is here. Joy in the full riches of my power and my strength. I am watching over you my beloved, my child.

October 30

* * *

To SENSE YOUR PRESENCE BECAUSE you are ever-present, to feel your love because we are your beloved, to see your hand in all that we encounter today whether I perceive it to be good or bad. To know you more because you are truth, you are light, you are goodness.

Draw me in O Lord, closer to thee I pray.

October 31

✳ ✳ ✳

"Blessed are those who have learned to acclaim you who walk in the light of your presence O Lord."

I am a child of the Most High God. I am his beloved. I am powerful because He is ALL-powerful. My trust and my faith is in you O Lord, all day long and into the night.

Write about it

Write about it

November 1

* * *

OPEN OUR EYES WIDER, OUR hearts deeper, our souls longing to know you more until we meet you in eternity.

So soon O Lord. Oh, so soon.

November 2

* * *

WE HAVE TO BE CAREFUL, watchful because even if our neighbors don't maintain their weeds they can silently creep over and begin to wrap themselves around the plants in our yard longing to recover from a hard winter and stunt, even halt their growth. Cut them away swiftly and carefully and do a thorough job even if the work was theirs to begin with, make it yours so that your plants will remain healthy, thriving is their goal.

November 3

∗ ∗ ∗

CLOTHE YOURSELVES AS GOD'S CHOSEN people wholly and dearly loved, with compassion, kindness, humility, gentleness and patience.

Colossians 3; 12

Quiet your mind.

Quiet my mind.

Goodness and Light:

To bloom and to grow to it's fullest potential the plant must be pruned.

November 4

* * *

WHAT IF EVERY PERSON YOU meet today is the key or clue to finding your purpose, the very reason for your existence on earth? What if every single second of today is planned specifically for you, detail by detail, custom made, laid out by God to assure His will be done? What if we knew the Creator of the Universe was living among us, that He was with us all of the time?

November 5

* * *

I BELIEVE THAT GOD IS the most powerful force in the Universe. I understand that surrender to self and a present mindedness that comes through discipline, prayer and meditation brings me closer to God. I know that we are all ONE and that un-forgiveness of another only betrays myself. The goal is to be more like the ONE who made me in His likeness, the ONE supreme God of the Universe.

November 6

* * *

SUCCESS IS TO KNOW LOVE because love is who we are and love is where we came from. Everything needed to emanate God and His light is within us. We were made whole, in His likeness. Our humanness, our environment takes us away from the whole, the source, God. It should be our mission to find it again through seeking God and His will for our lives.

I am whole made in His likeness.
I am love because He is love.
I am successful because I know what love is.
I am worthy because I am HIS.
God is LOVE and therefore so AM I!

November 7

* * *

I AM THANKFUL FOR THIS day O Lord. For knowing that it's not "about me." I am here on earth as a conduit of your love, to serve you and to serve others. I see you and feel you in the rising of the sun, bringing light and all the wonders of nature. I see you in it's setting, bringing dusk and lighting our skies with the moon and the stars. Thank you for light always present even in the darkest of days. Thank you for your love that penetrates even the hardest of hearts. Thank you for this amazing planet given us to live and thrive, to enjoy, and to learn from. I pray our eyes will open to your majesty and power. Help us to see you in the seconds of our days. I pray your will be done. Keep me surrendered O God, keep us close.

November 8

$*\ *\ *$

THANK YOU FOR HELPING ME to open my eyes to love instead of it's opposite, and for an understanding that in the beginning love is ALL and in the end LOVE is ALL.

God's love and ours

1 John 4; 7

November 9

* * *

THANKFUL FOR TODAY, FOR SURRENDER for healing, continue to bring me near to you O Lord, opening my eyes even wider to forgive, to love, to joy, to YOU.

Your will be done, this is my prayer.

November 10

✳ ✳ ✳

LORD THANK YOU FOR TODAY, opening my eyes, feeling refreshed, whole, loved and open to love. Thank you for teaching me that receiving is as important as giving because if I can't receive love then how can I fully give it?

I am strong through Him who strengthens me.
I am at peace because He lives in me.
I am love because I am made in His likeness and He is the great I AM.
God is LOVE, the source of ALL.

November 11

***

To see you O Lord, to open my eyes and see you.

This is my prayer.

Thanks be to God.

November 12

$* * *$

MY HEART BEATS BECAUSE OF you; I can place my hand over it and feel it's beating, our breath slowly and rhythmically moving without a thought from us. My eyes, gifts to see all of the beauty you place before us, unending, ever changing, landscapes that artists crave to imitate. We can taste foods, sweet and sour, savory and sublime. We can hear the cry of a baby and the crescendo of an orchestra, the melody of a songstress and the sweetness in our own child's voice. This O Lord is enough.

November 13

∗ ∗ ∗

THE SKIES, THE CLOUDS, STARS, sun and moon; Nature, teaches us, beckons us to see, to pay attention, what could be more important then the sight of a sunrise or sunset? The open sky full of light displaying colors, shades of blue and gray and white unabounding color, astonishing, alive, moving with the pulse of the Universe, in sync with all that is.

Our senses delight in the sounds of the seasons, dogs barking, water rushing, rain falling, our hearts beating along without a thought from us, slow and sure; puh pum, puh pum, puh pum.

Be still and sense the beating of your heart, dare to place your right hand over it and close your eyes and feel it. Our hearts beat with the pulse of the Universe.

"Taste and see that the Lord is good."

Psalm 19; 1-4

November 14

* * *

WE ARE CONNECTED LIKE THE ocean and the waves, like the birds and the sky, like trees to the earth, bound together by spirit, LOVE, never to part, sewn together.

Closer with thee O Lord, closer with thee.

November 15

✳ ✳ ✳

ANOTHER DAY TO LIVE COMES and goes so swiftly that we can hardly remember it. What stands out? The beauty you surround us with from dusk til dawn, a rainbow catches our attention, but what about clouds in the sky every day and at night? All day long and into the night we live and move and have our being because of you O Lord. The splendor of your love radiates from the earth surrounding us, absorbing us.

Open our eyes to see the work of your hands O Lord, to experience the work of your hands. Your will be done O Lord, not my will but thine be done forever and ever!

Thanks be to God!

Believe and receive.

November 16

KEEP US FOREVER THANKFUL. KEEP us forever humbled. Keep us in your care; drown us in your love.

November 17

* * *

WHAT GETS US EXCITED? WHAT do we care most about? What do we dream about? When we answer these questions we answer what IS our passion, our purpose the reason we are alive and were placed on earth to do and to experience. How do we get here?

Pray, "God, not my will but thine be done." Then learn to follow Him as He leads you.

Goodness and Light:

Quotes from some of the greatest teachers of our time:

Pay attention!

"The two most important days of your life...the day you are born and the day you find out why."

Mark Twain

"The best way to say "thank you God," is by letting go of the past and living in the present moment, right here and now."

Don Miguel Ruiz

"When you get, GIVE. When you learn, TEACH.

Maya Angelou

November 18

∗ ∗ ∗

WE ARE MADE IN YOUR likeness and you O Lord are love. We are living extensions of love originating from you, the very source of it. We then are here, on earth to represent YOU, to be whole, to show love, to focus on and remember from whence we came.

"For it is through you O Lord, I live and move and have my being."

I am, because you ARE the Great I AM.

God with us.

Everywhere!

Thanks be to God!

Amen

November 19

* * *

RECOGNIZING, KNOWING THAT IT TAKES discipline to remain focused on you no matter what!

Set my mind on you as I awaken, not allowing circumstances, frustrations, sickness or feelings, NOTHING or ANYTHING to take my focus away from my Creator, my GOD.

"Be joyful ALWAYS, pray continually, give thanks in ALL circumstances for this IS God's will for you in Christ Jesus. 1 Thessalonians 5 16-18

November 20

* * *

Breaking it down!

Be joyful always: our lives are a gift to be enjoyed, and if our faith is in God who gave us this gift, no matter what, we should remain joyful, understanding that He is in control of ALL.

Pray continually: remain connected to the source, which is God! Always focused on Him, communicating when we feel things are good or bad. He is the maker and the orchestrator of our lives and KNOWS what we need and when we need it.

Give thanks in ALL circumstances: Recognition, a KNOWING an honoring and respect of the fact that God is in control no matter what is happening! If we can humble ourselves to Him, He will bring us through anything and everything!

For this IS God's will for you in Christ Jesus: Our purpose will be unveiled, the closer we are to thee, the more our eyes will be opened to your will, our purpose our destiny.

November 21

✳ ✳ ✳

I SPEND A LOT OF time alone; I crave it, the quietness of being still because I KNOW I'm not alone. This is time where I can get understanding, fill up with goodness, put my mind on the right channel and adjust all of the settings. To be accepted, to be loved, to be understood, is something we all wish for and sometimes we do and say things we don't really believe to get them. It's not necessary because we are already accepted and loved and understood by you, our God.

It takes such strength and such reliance on our source to be who we are meant to be. Fully relying on God is an honorable goal, one worth giving all that we've got to give.

Thanks be to God!

Amen

November 22

* * *

THANK YOU LORD FOR YOUR light, beaming in all directions in our lives. Flowers and songs handpicked for me sent from a loving friend in Montana; a ticket to see my friends there; my girls and me going on an adventure to explore together, the ocean awaiting our arrival, the sand and sky.

Thank you Lord, that I can see you, you have taught me how to discern and focus on your light which covers all darkness. Surrendering, letting go brings such peace! Who knew that the wisdom that comes from closeness with you brings us closer to who we really are!

Being under water, holding our breath until our lungs ache and our heads feel as though they will burst and then we let go, feeling the breath of our bodies surging through our noses, our mouths, seeing the air bubbles as proof as we push to the surface with all that we are, opening our eyes, seeing the light that awaits us to burst through the surface and greet it. The pressure from our bodies, our heads slowly dissipating, the light warms us and assures us that we are ok.

Push to the surface of LIFE! Seek the light with all that you've got! Feel the warmth, the light the love that awaits us everyday, all day long, if we will just let go, stop holding our breath and trust.

November 23

$$* * *$$

SURRENDER TO HIM! COME TO the surface and breathe! Feel the warmth of God's spirit envelop your soul and rest. He IS capable! He created us! He is our Father! He wants us to swim through life surrendered to His power, our source for LOVE and all that is GOOD!

November 24

* * *

ALIVENESS; AWARENESS IS SUCH A miracle to behold! Seek it with ALL that you've got left.

I'm ALL in!

Thanks be to God!

November 25

THANK YOU FOR A GOOD night's rest, for Emily and Grace, for keeping them safe, protected mind, body and soul. Connection, one to the other to build each other up, understanding of feelings and when it is time to let go, always learning to let go and know that you are far more capable than I and you will take complete care of us ALL. Thanks be to God!

Amen

Goodness and Light:

Whatever it takes bring focus of my mind back to you, away from ego; self and back to LOVE.

November 26

* * *

KEEP ME FIRMLY IN YOUR light O Lord.

Amen

November 27

* * *

THANK YOU LORD FOR HOLDING us close, opening our eyes, even when we are fighting to keep them closed.

God with us.

Amen

November 28

* * *

I AM YOUR BELOVED CHILD. You chose me before the foundation of the world. I love you Lord. I'm thankful for times of struggle because I am humbled, I am learning humility and I am forever changed, again.

November 29

✳ ✳ ✳

I AM IN A NEW place and it is good. Be content, be thankful, and be quiet and watchful. Learn from your surroundings and grow as God waters you with His LOVE.

November 30

* * *

LIVING NEW, RECOGNIZING NEWNESS AND peace outside the walls I've built to hide behind, thinking they provide protection but really they hold me back and keep me from experiencing the perfect will of God the Father. Stepping out; experiencing freedom, the air is different, it's easier to breathe it but painstakingly hard to move away from beliefs held all of my life that were false, untrue. Reminding myself what IS true completely dependent on God to continue walking, the journey never ends because the goal is to know you more but to know you completely is impossible. So we keep on walking doing our best remaining thankful, humble and with our eyes on you. Love and Light brings you to me. "come near to me and I will come near to you."

Thanks be to God!

Amen

Write about it

_____

_____

_____

_____

_____

_____

_____

_____

_____

_____

_____

_____

_____

_____

_____

_____

_____

_____

_____

_____

_____

_____

_____

_____

_____

_____

Write about it

December 1

* * *

ENERGIZE ME O LORD TO do your will. Put a fire in me a burning desire to seek my purpose, whatever it takes, make me strong, keep me focused on you, perseverance, patience, trust, faith.

You are love and you are light, "the Way the truth and the LIFE."

Thanks be to God!

December 2

* * *

THE TRUTH IS I AM made perfect in your likeness and I am completely and wholly LOVED. You are LOVE and therefore so AM I!

Thanks be to God!

Believe and receive!

December 3

* * *

I AM WEAK BUT HE is strong.

I know that you know our needs O Lord and you will meet them abundantly. Thank you for Emily and Grace, for hope. Thank you for creativeness, for uniqueness for imagination. Closer to thee O Lord, this is my prayer, may I come closer with thee. I'm walking with you into a new land for which I am destined to BE. Teach me, show me, and keep me near, my focus on you all day long.

Thanks be to God!

Amen

December 4

Be transformed

IT IS MY CHOICE TO feel sad, a learned behavior from my past. Even if things are happening in my life that feel sad, I can choose to feel joyful because God is in control of the seconds and minutes and hours of my day. I have to have faith that when my circumstances appear "sad" it is so that I will learn to be content and joyful anyway. Learn from these times and know that life has ebbs and flows. There's a reason and a season for ALL and my faith my hope is in you O Lord. I smile today and keep my focus on you and your promises because I know you have my best interests in store and that you love me with an un-imaginable love. Thank you for keeping us close even when we fall away. You are here and I am forever thankful for you.

Thanks be to God!

Amen

December 5

* * *

TODAY IS A NEW DAY! Open my mind to receive love, to receive newness to receive knowledge and wisdom, always growing in faith and hope! Praying to feel the joy that can only come from relationship with you. Forgive me for not trusting in the plan you have laid out for me. Forgive me for feeling sorry for myself, an old behavior that is hard to release. FREE me from it O Lord! FILL me with your light, your joy your peace and ultimately your truth.

Thanks be to God!

Amen

2 Samuel 22; 29

"You are my lamp O Lord, the Lord turns my darkness into light."

December 6

∗ ∗ ∗

I AM THANKFUL FOR TODAY, for time with Emily and Grace. Wading through the hurt to get to the truth and your light, Lord. Thank you for helping me push through the hurt and pain, thank you for healing old wounds. Thank you for helping me, teaching me to see it's up to me and my dependence on you that will determine whether or not they will remain closed, heal and even disappear leaving no scars behind.

Lord, continue to help me to rise above, to stand tall because I am your beloved. I am made in your likeness. I am because you are the GREAT I AM. I am thankful for your nearness, I will continually seek your Will for it is "through you I live and move and have my being."

Amen

December 7

* * *

I AM ALIVE IN CHRIST! We are works of art fashioned by God our Father! Praise thee O Lord for your sovereignty, your power, and your artistry, your Greatness! I am because you are the GREAT I AM! I am alive and well!

Thanks be to God!

Amen

Made alive in Christ!

Ephesians 2

December 8

* * *

LOVE ONE ANOTHER. DID YOU know that you are one of a kind? There is no one else like you? Your fingerprint is yours and your alone, like no one else's in the whole wide world. You are ONE of a kind! What is special about you? What is your favorite color? Do you like to paint with your fingers or with a brush? Do you like to doodle?

If you were walking and you came upon a tree that was easy to climb, would you climb it?

Thank you Lord for today, for life for love for your presence. Keep us focused on you and your good and perfect Will for our walk towards heaven. Help us to remain in you.

God with us.

Thanks be to God.

Amen

December 9

LOVE ONE ANOTHER. SEE PAST self, be compassionate towards others; be kind; learn; smile; laugh; we are alive and well.

Thank you Lord for watching over us for keeping us safe. I pray for your protection over Emily and Grace today as they travel. I know that you have ALL under control and your good and perfect will, WILL be done!

Thanks be to God!

Amen

December 10

* * *

REMAINING IN THANKFULNESS, STARTING WITH today, counting my blessings. Relying, resting in God to sustain me to nurture me to love me to provide for me. Focusing on God and His word and His Holy Spirit within me. God is my foundation; unmovable; impenetrable, upon which I WILL build my house according to his plan, His Will.

December 11

* * *

I FEEL LIKE I'M CRYING out for help and not being heard, I am lonely and afraid. Forgive me Lord and keep me safe, my trust is in you all day long. I will persevere, this is God's plan and He is my Father and I am his beloved. He will walk me through and I will be better for it, stronger and more wise.

I pray your Will be done no matter what it takes. I am yours.

Isaiah 12; 2

December 12

✳ ✳ ✳

I AM THANKFUL FOR TODAY, thankful for your love. I am thankful for trials that make us stronger, more compassionate, humbled and wise. I am thankful for the light of God shining more brightly every day. I am thankful for courage and boldness in the face of adversity. I am thankful for the ability to learn and for teachers. I am thankful that I am not blind and that I can see. I am thankful for my home, for safety and security and protection. I am thankful for my relationship with you, God, knowing you will never leave me nor forsake me. Thanks be to God.

Amen

December 13

* * *

TODAY I AM THANKFUL THAT I am learning to live in today, the now. I am thankful that I can accept forgiveness and responsibility for my part in the play. To be better than I was yesterday, to see what I am meant to see, to live the life I'm meant to lead, to expect miracles every second of the day, to know the power of God is in control of my life, for these things, I remain in gratitude and thanks.

Not my will but thine be done, I am weak but you O Lord are strong.

Thanks be to God.

Amen

December 14

∗ ∗ ∗

THANK YOU LORD FOR TODAY, for your loving care. I pray your Will be done. I know you have us in your care. Thanks be to God.

Amen

December 15

* * *

THANK YOU LORD FOR TODAY, for the chance to see you more, to be closer with thee. It is true, your presence is evident all around us but we must pay close attention. It's not easy in to-day's world with all the distractions, provided us that draw us in keep us from you. Thank you for hope and healing Lord. Thank you for discipline and lessons learned. It's never easy but always worth it, you O Lord are worth everything. You O Lord gave us life and if we remain surrendered to you we will see your plan for living it. I draw my strength from you, you are the source, the light, and the foundation, and without you I am nothing, useless. With you I am everything.

Thanks be to God.

Amen

December 16

JESUS IS GOD'S LIGHT, SHINING brightly for us to follow. We are a reflection of God's light. Shine brightly because we are made in His likeness and we are his beloveds. Lord, thank you for today, for healing, for refreshment, for love. I don't need my eyes to see you but I'm glad they've been opened, I didn't know just how closed they were. I thought when I was awake and my eyes open, I could see you but you showed me otherwise, my eyes were opened but I was seeing through myself. Thank you for lifting a veil I didn't know was there. Thank you that your light shines brighter than ever! Thank you for loving me through, keeping me close, disciplining me more. I am weak but you O Lord are strong. I am yours and I pray your Will be done.

Amen

December 17

✳ ✳ ✳

THANK YOU FOR TODAY. THANK your for healing and hope. Thank you for renewing our minds. Thank you for love, thank you for your light. Thank you for your strength, thank you for everything! How delicate and fragile life is. I'm learning to be thankful for simple blessings that really aren't that simple. I am thankful for waking up with clarity of mind, for awareness and present mindedness, for relationships and connection for understanding and being able to feel again. I am thankful to feel my fingers on this pen, to hear the fan and feel its wind, to see and touch my dog and my cat and really be present with them. To notice my breath and how it feels, rhythmically moving through my body all day long, to really taste my food.

Keep me here O Lord, keep me near I pray your Will be done. It's the reason I'm here. Thank you Lord for your love. I praise thee and thank thee all day long.

Thanks be to God.

Amen

December 18

* * *

THANK YOU FOR TODAY, FOR a good night's rest. I am completely surrendered to you and know that your perfect Will, will be done. Forgive me of my humanness and continue to teach and discipline me. Thank you for life for health for love. You show up all day long when we are paying attention, you really are everywhere, the Alpha, the Omega, the beginning and the end. We cannot hide from the love of God.

Thanks be to God.

Amen

December 19

∗ ∗ ∗

GOD WITH US, EVERY SINGLE day all day long and into the night. Show me the way I should go, for to you I lift up my soul. Thank you Lord for today. I am ready. I know that you are with me guiding me, keeping me close. No matter what it takes, my trust is in you O Lord all day long and into the night. You are here; you will never leave us nor forsake us. You are love and so am I.

Thanks be to God.

Amen

Psalm 32; 8

I will instruct you and teach you in the way you should go. I will counsel you and watch over you.

Jeremiah 29; 13

You will seek me and find me when you seek me with all of your heart.

Psalm 143; 8

Let the morning bring me word of your unfailing love for I have put my trust in you.

December 20

* * *

HOPE IS OUR ANCHOR TO God in heaven. Faith, hope and love, our armor against all who come against us. Focus on God's continual presence and the hope of heaven. I AM releasing self-centeredness; help us to regard the other before ourselves. Knowing that if my circumstances were the same I might react the same, therefore we are all connected one in the same, our life experience unique yet our dependence and belief in God or a higher power determining perspective and purpose. Surrender to self and continually rise to the call of our destiny, God's will takes courage and discipline, but faith and hope and focus on Him will bring us to it and through it. Closer to thee I pray.

Amen

December 21

$*\ *\ *$

THANK YOU FOR YOUR UNFAILING word, for your unfailing love. Thank you for today and ALL that is in it. Thank you for truth and the courage to do my best to live in it, even though it can be really hard and really hurt. Thank you for the forgiveness of sins, knowing that you know my heart despite my ego. You have freed us from the chains of our past, we must have the courage, the boldness to take steps and follow you. Keep our eyes on you O Lord. Keep us seeking, searching, being; now, today.

Thy will be done.

Amen

December 22

✳ ✳ ✳

HOPE LIKE AN ANCHOR, OUR lifeline to God. God is the anchor of our souls. God's greatest commandment is to "love the Lord your God with all your heart, with all your strength and with all your mind." And the next greatest commandment is to "love your neighbor as yourself."

Goodness and Light

Agapao or Agape means, commitment of devotion that is directed by the will and can be commanded as a duty. Agape IS love, all encompassing, it's like when we jump in a pool and we are engulfed with water, there's nothing the water isn't touching. We are completely covered, saturated in the LOVE of God.

December 23

* * *

THANK YOU FOR TODAY, FOR health for healing. Thank you for
teaching and the ability to learn and grow towards you. Seek
and we shall find you, knock and you will open the door. I
pray my mind will remain on goodness and love, that I will be
thoughtful when I feel hurt or offended and ask, "what would
Jesus do?" that I will treat others the way I myself wish to be
treated, that I will find strength in knowing my Father, God
is here and will sustain me and comfort me and love me. I am
his beloved and He is my strength and my redeemer, my rock
and my fortress that cannot be shaken, He IS immovable. That
is God Almighty! I pray to remain close to you Lord, my mind
and soul tethered to you. Thank you Lord, for you are everything, you are ALL!

Thanks be to God!

Amen

December 24

* * *

THANK YOU FOR TODAY. I am thankful for life and for learning, for being. You are goodness and love; our minds must remain focused on you and your word at all times. Pray continually, knowing that your power is infinite and mighty. We must surrender our day our lives to you. You will not disappoint! God is the Alpha and the Omega, the beginning and the end. His love endures forever! God is the way, the truth and the LIFE.

Believe and receive His promises!

Amen

December 25

✳ ✳ ✳

GOD WITH US. PEACE BE with you. Thank you for today, thank you for opening my heart and my mind to receive your word, your promises to grow my faith in the unseen, to build trust by connecting to the source of all things. Thank you for writing and what it's been for me in my life, I pray I can encourage others through it. I know as long as I remain close to thee you will show me the way, your will shall be done and I will experience your peace and love, your joy even when my circumstances seem hard. Thank you for loving us so, for pulling us back to you for knowing what's best and guiding us to it.

Thanks be to God.

Amen

Psalm 121

December 26

∗ ∗ ∗

I AM THANKFUL TODAY FOR life, for a peaceful home for beautiful people in my life. I am thankful for teachers and the ability to learn and grow and the willingness to seek your Will everyday. I am thankful and humbled by you O Lord, by your Holy Spirit and by the example of your son Jesus Christ.

Keep us humble, keep us close, and keep us focused on you until the day we meet again. We forget how quickly the days are passing, melting away filled with busyness. Things that matter not filling our precious time here on earth, awaken us O Lord in spirit and in love.

Amen

December 27

∗ ∗ ∗

RELEASING ALL UNFORGIVENESS, I AM love. I am being infiltrated with your goodness, love, joy, peace, patience, kindness, gentleness and self-control. I am Love. Opening up, seeing myself as connected to all of creation, a part of, not separate from the work of your hands. Seeking to understand and know the ONE who is all-powerful all knowing, the ONE who is ALL, He who controls and orchestrates ALL. The painting of our lives filled with color, exhibiting pain endured, hope and faith to overcome, trust as we surrender and victory in the light of His love.

God is the artist, the conductor, the Master Gardener who longs for his masterpiece, his work, his creation to reflect Him because it came from HIS perfect hands. God, the author and perfector of our faith.

We are a canvas splattered with lovely colors symbolizing pain and joy, peace and grace. No two paintings alike, all part of a series called connection, more enlightened as a whole making sense in the same exhibit. The light jumping off the canvas, overshadowing darkness every single time! Togetherness, wholeness, ONE is the theme, LOVE is the source, the light is the miracle.

December 28

***

BE JOYFUL ALWAYS; PRAY CONTINUALLY, for this is God's will in Christ Jesus.

Be completely devoted to me, utterly trust in me, and be wholly focused on me. You are my beloved whom I adore and whom I gift with overflowing abundance. See me.

December 29

* * *

THANK YOU LORD FOR TODAY. Praying for all who are hurting, may they put their trust, their hope their faith in you and you alone.

I am special and feel your love. Thank you Lord for hope and peace, for relationship with you. Thank you for pulling me close, for your miracles.

December 30

* * *

PEACE BE STILL. THANK YOU for today, for blessings for peace for protection. Thank you for stillness, quietness, for time to spend with you each morning. I see you in everything, in everyone. Continue to make me and mold me, continue to love me and show me. Make me courageous and bold that your Will be done. Love lives, love never dies. You are love. God is love.

Amen

December 31

* * *

AND IN THE END, SHE discovered there was nothing to be afraid
of...

They discovered there is nothing to fear, they are free to give
and to receive love and no one is above or below the other.
They were all created to live in harmony forever, connected,
held together by the strength and power of their creator, the
ultimate source of love the spirit of God Almighty.

Write about it

Write about it

I WENT ALL MY LIFE not knowing that I AM the light, we are the light of God's eye, the light of all creation! Thank God, we know it now!

Thank you for today O Lord. You light up my life just knowing that you are in control of today. You have all under control. Praise thee O Lord, thank you for love, peace and hope. Thank you for growing our faith, showing us your miracles every day, all day long.

Keep us in tune with the symphony of life with you as the conductor, who perfectly orchestrates the ebbs and flows that deepen into crescendo and ultimately brings everyone to their feet to applaude and praise the work of your hands. You are the master of our universe; help us to listen intently for the melody, for the sound of each instrument, all, important and necessary for the score to be played with perfection. *Peace be with you.* Peace be with us. Receive His grace and peace today.

Thanks be to God.

Amen

I want to share what I believe to be God's Will for my life. My very purpose as I walk this earth. You will see as you continue seeking, that God's Will for our lives tends to expand and grow as we follow Him. I have come to understand that we are the ones who stop the growth, I believe God will continue to grow us closer to Him until our dying day, until we meet soul to soul and are united in spirit, ONE, for eternity.

God's Will for my life is first, for me to give to others what I wished to receive when I was at my lowest. This means to me that when I encounter someone who is struggling I can meet them right where they are and love them anyway, no judgment, just being there for them and sharing what God has done for me and in turn what He can do for them. I am able to practice this daily through my job as a therapist.

I am to be a conduit of love and light for others to see that it's ok to open their thought processes, their minds eye to new or different ways of living their lives and not be held captive to a "false self," living what others have told them they are all of their lives. Re-connecting to spirit, to whom God created them to be, not what the world thinks they should be.

I am to appropriate an understanding that we can discipline our minds in order to harness our thoughts and see only God and His goodness and all of the gifts that He provides. The miracles of God are here, now, all around us, every day.

I am a seeker and a writer of divinely appointed prayers and teachings and I must remain focused on the ONE who speaks through me, God Almighty. I am to remain present minded, awake and aware, paying attention to Him through spending time with him, meditating, praying and especially journaling, a gift given me as a little girl, something that gives me joy and peace and now is being used to shine the light on my Father, my God.

My prayer for you:

I pray that your eyes are opened, that you will continue seeking God's perfect WILL for your life.

I pray that you will seek the light in your day; it's always there. Light covers darkness, every single time.

I pray that you will believe and receive the miracles that await you every single day when you choose to seek goodness and live in thankfulness.

I pray for the awareness that the gift of God's Will is truly the greatest gift we WILL ever receive!

I pray most of all; you will be found, always praying "not my will but thine be done."

"I once was lost but now I'm found, was blind but now I see."

Blessings, LOVE and Light.

www.ingramcontent.com/pod-product-compliance
Lightning Source LLC
Chambersburg PA
CBHW031824090426
42741CB00005B/117

* 9 7 8 0 6 9 2 3 9 4 6 5 6 *